FOR THOSE WHO SEE

For Those Who See

M. B. TERRY

C-PIN Publishing

For all those who believe.
For all those who do not.

FOR THOSE WHO SEE
© Copyright 2022 by M. B. Terry
This book is a work of fiction. Names, characters, places, and events are the product of the author's imagination or are used fictitiously. Any resemblance to actual events, locations, or persons, living or dead, is coincidental.
Trademarks: This book identifies personal names, product names, and services known to be trademarks, registered trademarks, or service marks of their respective holders. The author acknowledges the trademark status in this work of fiction. The publication and use of these trademarks are not authorized, associated with, or sponsored by the trademark owners.
The scanning, uploading, and distribution without permission is a theft of the author's intellectual property. Reproduction for review purposes is permitted. If you would like permission for any other material in this book, please email: forthosewhosee@outlook.com.
The author is not responsible for websites or other disparaging posts or content not produced by the author or a representative.
ISBN: 978-0-578-37469-7

Chapter 1

IN PLAIN SIGHT

The frigid wind grabbed the door, and Maxwell tightened his grip on the handle for a quick close. It was cold and windy outside, and everyone in the coffee shop looked up as if his entrance had deeply annoyed them.

The room was much like every other coffee shop, filled with people on their devices, silent, looking down with their faces highlighted by a soft, electronic glow. Large couches and oversized chairs were placed throughout, and local art hung on the walls. A small copper serving counter was along the back wall, positioned between three vintage, tiled tables. To the right of that was a fireplace.

A young couple softly spoke in one corner as they held each other's hand. A fat black cat was curled up, sleeping on a stack of oversized books. A sign on the fireplace mantle read, "*The cats' names are Ratdog and Phineas.*" Maxwell wasn't sure if the plump feline was Ratdog or Phineas, and where the other cat was, was anyone's guess.

The place smelled of coffee, gingerbread, and cinnamon. A low chatter filled the air. He liked the shop. It was unassuming and welcoming.

Maxwell scanned the room and caught the eye of a girl staring at him as she sat cross-legged in one of the overstuffed chairs on the far wall. She seemed to hold his gaze for a moment then quickly darted her eyes downward.

He decided to make himself comfortable, so he walked over to the hat rack, took off his apricot scarf and black pea coat, and then slowly approached the counter while peering sideways into a mirror. He ordered a peach tea then settled into a worn, leather chair to the girl's right. He lowered himself and noticed that the girl was reading *The Da Vinci Code* and that she looked up every time the door was opened, as if she were expecting someone.

The barista called his name and motioned to him with a nod that his order was ready. He got up, grabbed the cup, and then sat back down. He took a sip of his peach tea, peering over the rim to glance at the girl again. She was stunningly beautiful.

His thoughts were soon interrupted by the sound of wood scraping across the floor. An old man with a leathered face and squinty eyes, wearing a heavy wool cap and a large, wool, blue sweater, dragged a small stool into the center of the room. Maxwell remembered a sign on the door that said tonight was poetry night. He shifted his attention to the reader.

The old man cleared his throat then began. "This poem is titled *Fishing with Frank Mundus* …

> "*Fishing with a legend,*
> *Is not an easy time,*
> *Leaning against the gunwale,*
> *Banging against the chine …*"

Maxwell glanced at the girl again, pretending to read the specials board behind her. She looked up and caught his eye.

The old man continued in his shaky, aging, baritone voice, his words wafting through the room.

> "*Wiry stature, weathered face,*
> *Hell in his eyes,*

Little patience or grace ...
Chum, chum, chum, that is what we will do.
Do not look up ... Captain Mundus is staring at you."

Great, Maxwell thought, *it's a poem about staring at somebody*. He realized then how awkward he must appear to the girl.

"Ever alert for a fish he hates,
To show itself and take the bait.
Chum, chum, chum, that is what we will do.
Don't look up ... Captain Mundus is peering at you."

Maxwell shifted in his chair, took another sip of his peach tea, and thought about the best way to approach the girl without appearing forward. She was so beautiful that he knew he had to ask for her name and not miss this opportunity. Even a soft rejection would be acceptable.

The older man continued after a brief pause to clear his throat.

"The click of the reel,
Then wire peel, the dragging rate.
Shouts, confusion,
The fish fighting, fighting to alter its fate."

The old man looked up to receive the response as a smattering of applause broke the silence of the room.

That was a great poem, Maxwell thought as he clapped and remembered the time when he had gone fishing for big-eye tuna out of Montauk on the charter boat, Bronco Explorer II. The nights had been eerie, drifting under the stars in Block Canyon, in complete silence and surrounded by a wall of the blackest night. The days had been filled with the lull of big game fishing until the words "fish on" had been shouted from the tuna tower.

Maxwell wanted to approach the girl but grew nervous, feeling as if his stomach were tied in a knot. He felt something,

something that he hadn't felt before—a strange and welcoming feeling.

Finally, he stood up, took a deep breath, and began walking toward her. When he was a few steps away, she looked up, as if instantly annoyed by his approach, and then she looked back down at the book.

Deflated, he managed to mutter a soft, "Hello."

She glanced up again. "Hi."

"I couldn't help but notice that you are reading *The Da Vinci Code*." His voice slightly trembled as he spoke.

"Yes." She shifted her posture once more, and the overhead lighting highlighted her porcelain face, long brown hair, and deep blue eyes as she looked up at him once again. She was wearing a white sweater, accented with a small diamond cross pendant. He detected a foreign accent.

"Where are you from?" he asked.

"Southwold, United Kingdom." She delicately whisked a sprig of her light brown hair from the frame of her blue-rimmed glasses. "I read the book some time ago, but with all of this new interest in searching for the holy relics in this world, I decided to reread it."

"I read it, also, a while back because I am drawn to ancient history."

She shifted again in the chair, and he sensed she was growing a little uncomfortable, so he decided to change the topic.

"Do you come here often?"

"Occasionally, when they have poetry night."

"I come here occasionally, too," Maxwell said. "I love the peach tea, and I signed up for a poetry class, so I figured this is a good place to meet people with similar interests. People who drink coffee and tea write poetry."

That was stupid to say, he thought.

She looked up, probably to see if he was serious. "Peach tea," she repeated in a faint whisper as a small, coy smile lit up her face.

After a few seconds of awkward silence, he decided to return to his chair.

"Okay then, see you around." The feeling of defeat engulfed him as he started to walk away.

"Hey, peach tea drinker ... if you are into unsolved ancient mysteries, have you ever heard of Newport Tower in Rhode Island?"

Maxwell turned around. "No."

"Look it up if you're interested in that ancient history, mystery thing."

Maxwell sat down in the overstuffed leather chair and immediately replayed the conversation in his mind, reviewing her body language and what had been said, as if watching the rerun of a bad movie. *I am such an idiot*, he thought. *Do real men even drink peach tea?*

He began thinking about how his little sister, Laurel, had gotten him started on it. He would drink peach tea with her and talk about life. He enjoyed the conversations. She was much younger than him—they were a good ten years apart—but his parents always insisted that she had been planned. Maxwell adored her and was genuinely interested in her ideas, goals, and life as a girl in Generation Y.

I should've told her the story behind the tea more, he thought.

Embarrassed, Maxwell finished the tea then decided to leave. He looked over at the girl once more. She was back to reading her book.

He grabbed his coat and scarf then headed for the exit, trying to hide his embarrassment while passing her once more, but when he opened the door to leave, he tripped on the doormat.

"Figures," he muttered, hoping the girl had not noticed.

He realized he had forgotten to ask for her name as he drove away.

Maxwell could not wait to get home and research Newport Tower. If she had asked him about it, she must be interested. It could be a good way to connect with her.

He realized that he had never felt like this before. There was something about her.

Arriving at his apartment, he threw his keys on the table, sat down at his computer, and began to research Newport Tower. He soon learned that it was a stone structure in Touro Park, Newport, Rhode Island, shrouded in decades of controversy of who had constructed it and when. He was amazed at the amount of information available. There was even a small museum dedicated to it.

As he read, he was reminded of roaming the dunes behind his family's restaurant on the east end of Long Island in Napeague. He thought of all the old bottles and bullets that he had recovered there and the pair of teeth that he had found that he had imagined belonging to an unfortunate shipwreck victim. His father had called in local archeologists, who had determined that the teeth had belonged to a pig. It had been his first big yet uneventful find. He had spent the next ten years roaming the dunes of Napeague, looking, searching. Those early adventures had sparked his interest in archaeology and had inspired him to major in it at New York State University at Stony Brook.

***

The next morning, Maxwell continued his research on Newport Tower before he had to leave for class. He came across an interesting publication on Google Books titled *The Old Stone Mill, Newport R.I.* written by Charles Timothy Brooks. The book outlined an argument against the claims that the tower had been built as a mill, which turned out to be a decades-old controversy.

At the site, Mr. Brooks claimed that coins dating from Henry II, with the year 1160, had been found, along with complicated aqueducts connected to a more extensive complex development that was pinned to the Norse or Northmen, as he described the people.

He supported his theory by pointing out the absence of buried bodies, which he attributed to the custom of burning the dead by Northmen. Most compelling was his linking of the inscriptions on Dighton Rock and Pakwewatanis, near Mt. Holyoke in New England, said to be of ancient origin.

Maxwell could not believe it. For years, his uncle, who lived on the east end of Long Island, had claimed that there were areas on the beach where hundreds of boulders and rocks were inscribed, some with ancient hieroglyphs. If the people who had created these inscriptions had been on Rhode Island, they had also most likely been on Long Island. Could he be right?

Maxwell made a mental note to visit him.

He continued to read.

> On the ancient structure in Newport, there are no ornaments remaining, which might, possibly, have served to guide us in assigning the probable date of its erection. I am persuaded that all who are familiar with old Northern architecture will concur, that this building WAS ERECTED AT A PERIOD DECIDEDLY NOT LATER than the XIIth century.

Wow, what a claim, Maxwell thought.

What he read next made him most excited.

Mr. Brooks believed that Newport Tower had been a sacred destination and belonged to some monastery or Christian place of worship in one of the chief parishes in Vinland.

This is amazing, Maxwell thought. Was this structure an ancient monastery or a place of worship, built here or moved from another site? He was determined to try to find out and immerse himself in the subject in hopes of meeting the girl again.

Chapter 2

DISCOVERY

Maxwell could not get the girl at the coffee shop out of his mind. He thought about her constantly, recanting the short conversation they'd had. He began going back to the coffee shop daily, at the same time, to try to see her again.

He had almost given up until, one day, his luck changed. He walked in, brushed the snow off his coat, and glanced around, expecting a disappointing void, yet there she was, sitting in the same overstuffed chair on the back wall, reading a book.

Maxwell gasped as his nerves began to overtake him, and then he started sweating as he walked to the counter to order. He tried to maintain his composure.

"May I help you?" the barista asked.

"Yes, *Dan*," Maxwell said as he glanced at the barista's nametag.

There was a long, uncomfortable pause as he silently debated whether to order the peach tea or opt for something more masculine. The barista began looking around impatiently. Maxwell started to feel the pressure.

"I will ha-a-a-ave ... um ... th-the ... peach tea." He had realized that the tea would be a great conversation starter with the girl.

He waited at the counter for the barista to hand him the mug. Then he decided to approach her.

"Hello again," he said as he walked over to the same oversized leather chair to her right.

She looked up. "Oh, hi."

As his thoughts went blank, he stood there, nervously staring at her.

Finally, she spoke. "Peach tea?"

"Yes," he managed to mutter.

She smiled again. "Me, too. It's delicious."

With those words, a weight was lifted off Maxwell's body. He sat down in the chair, crossed his legs, and regained a little more confidence.

"You know, I never did ask you your name."

"It's Mary. Yours?"

"Maxwell."

"Nice to meet you," they both said at the same time.

"You know," Maxwell said, "I researched Newport Tower you told me about and found some amazing facts and literature on the subject."

Mary immediately perked up. She put her book and glasses on the side table and leaned toward Maxwell. "Continue. What did you find?"

"Well, I found an old book online by a fellow named Brooks who disputes the old mill rumor spread by Benedict Arnold, the governor of the island in the 1600s who claimed he had built it. Mr. Brooks connected the origin of the tower to the twelfth century. Another fellow, named Dr. J. F. Allen, found that the dimensions of the tower were remarkably like a church in the United Kingdom."

Maxwell could tell Mary was intrigued.

Mary smiled. "Do you want to meet later for lunch or dinner to discuss this? I must go to class, and I don't like discussing these matters in such an exposed area."

"Sure." Maxwell was elated. He could not believe that Mary had asked him out.

Wait—what class was she speaking about? What did she study? He had so many questions.

He decided to take a chance and invite her over to his apartment for lunch to show her the book that he had found online. However, he knew it was unlikely that she would accept the invitation.

"My place for lunch? Around noon?" he asked.

There was a long pause as Mary assessed him. She looked him up and down, hesitated, and then accepted. "Sure, see you then. Here is my number. Text me the address."

***

Just after twelve, Mary arrived, carrying a large backpack. She seemed excited.

"What are we having? I don't think I mentioned I'm a vegetarian."

"No, you didn't. I could run next store and order a large salad at The Roll."

"Great," Mary said.

Maxwell was so excited that he did not think twice about leaving her in the apartment alone. However, on the way to the restaurant, he had second thoughts about it as he tried to convince himself that she was not the type who would steal. There was nothing of sizeable monetary value in his apartment, anyway; just sentimental artifacts that he had recovered over time, mismatched thrift store furniture, and a few plants that were in desperate need of TLC.

He returned to his apartment fifteen minutes later, out of breath and with a large salad. As he entered, he noticed Mary standing in front of a bookshelf, looking at something that she held in her hand. He hoped she did not notice the layers of dust.

"Where did you get these old bullets and bottles?" she asked as she slowly placed a small brass bullet back on the shelf.

"Oh, I collected them in Napeague when I was a boy, where my family has a restaurant."

"They are fascinating," she replied.

Mary took a large, faded book out of her backpack and carefully placed it on the coffee table in front of the couch. It's worn leather rubbed red on her hands.

"I see you brought an old book," Maxwell noted.

"Yes, it's titled *Broader Views of Britain Photographic Views of the New World*. It has a photo of Newport Tower. Come over here; I'll show you." She carefully turned to a marked page, showing a photograph of the tower captioned, "*The Round Tower at Newport*." She began to study the photo.

"Oh, my word," Mary said. "The text pokes fun at the Americans. It says here, '*It is one of the few ancient relics about which Americans have already succeeded in bewildering themselves …*'" Mary looked up in apology. "The text mentions the Norsemen and the dispute of its origin."

"Why do you have that book, and where did you get it?" Maxwell asked as he handed her a cup of peach tea.

"It was my great-grandmother's. She handed it down to my grandmother, and then my mum inherited it. My father told me that my mum said there was always a letter accompanying it with symbols and strange writing that my great-grandmother had produced through her research and the first line was, '*For those who see.*' That is all she could remember … or so she said. You see, this page of the tower has been marked. I promised my grandmother that I would continue her work on it. This is the first time I really have any interest in it, though."

Mary slowly scanned the page then took some photos with her phone. "Can I email these to you so that we can bring them up on the computer over there?" She gestured to Maxwell's computer by the front window.

"Sure." He gave her his email address then walked over to the computer to turn it on.

Mary took more photos between bites of her salad, sent them to the address, and then walked over to where Maxwell was sitting. She pulled up a chair close to him, and his heart started to race. He could smell her perfume. Distracted, he fumbled around with his mouse, trying to open the photos.

"If you think these photos of the tower are important, we should study it and view it left to right in sections, like a grid," he said.

They marked some areas of interest where the rocks that made up the tower changed, but nothing was evident.

A little disappointed, Mary muttered, *"For those who see."* She returned to finishing her salad, standing behind Maxwell.

Suddenly, Mary dropped her fork, which clattered across the floor. She was staring at the computer screen from the center of the room. "Maxwell!" she exclaimed. "There is a lion on the tower!"

"What?"

"There is a lion image, a figure on the tower near the upper left of the window," she said excitedly. "It looks like a mosaic."

Maxwell could not see it, so he rose from his chair and walked to where Mary stood, thinking the depth would help. He could not believe his eyes. A subtle change in the stone alignment formed a circle that looked like a mane, an eye, and the mouth of a lion. Only half the head was visible.

Mary looked at Maxwell. *"For those who see ..."* she said, her voice barely a whisper.

They spent the next hour researching the tower on the internet to see if there was any mention of a lion or any other symbol on websites or in books. They came up empty.

"In my research, I found that Newport Tower once had stucco and vines covering the walls. That's why it could have been missed—cloaked in obscurity for all these years." Maxwell was excited about the discovery, but soon the obligations of school crept back into his mind.

Mary went back to look at the photo in her book again and mentioned that there was no evidence of stucco or vines in the 1895 photograph.

"I am so sorry, Mary, but it is getting late, and I have to study for an anthropology test. I'll drive you home," Maxwell said.

Mary looked him up and down, and Maxwell expected that she would reject his offer. After all, they had only just met. Instead, Mary said, "Okay, I have class tomorrow, too. Let's keep this between us. Can you drive me to my girlfriend's house? It's nearby."

Maxwell agreed with a slight nod.

As he drove her home, it grew dark, and as he glanced her way, he could see flashing glimpses of her beauty as the headlights of passing cars illuminated her.

"Do you want to meet again tomorrow?" Maxwell asked as he slowly pulled the car into her friend's driveway.

"Sure," Mary agreed.

"When can I pick you up?"

"I have class until three thirty. How about after then?"

"Okay, I'll pick you up at four."

Maxwell walked Mary to the door, where he nervously shook her hand and said goodbye. Then he walked back to his car.

As he was driving to his apartment, he passed a car that quickly hit the brakes, casting a red glow in the evening light, and then made a U-turn. The car was behind him now.

That's odd, Maxwell thought, thinking it might be a police officer. *I'm not speeding.*

The car was gaining on him, forcing him to speed up. He decided to cut through the Stony Brook campus, and as he turned into it, the car continued going straight.

He relaxed.

***

The next day after class, Maxwell picked Mary up and drove her to his apartment to continue talking about the discovery. She was excited, talking the entire way about the book and the lion head on the tower. She sounded like she was trying to convince herself more and more of what they had seen.

"Would you like some tea?" Maxwell asked when they stepped inside his apartment.

"Sure."

Maxwell went into the kitchen, and as he was filling the kettle, Mary called him back into the living room, where she was sitting at the computer. As he sat down next to her, she pointed to a figure above the lion's head and slightly to the right.

"This looks like some sort of cat," she exclaimed. "Do you see it? The dark stones form two ears, and the light stone forms the face."

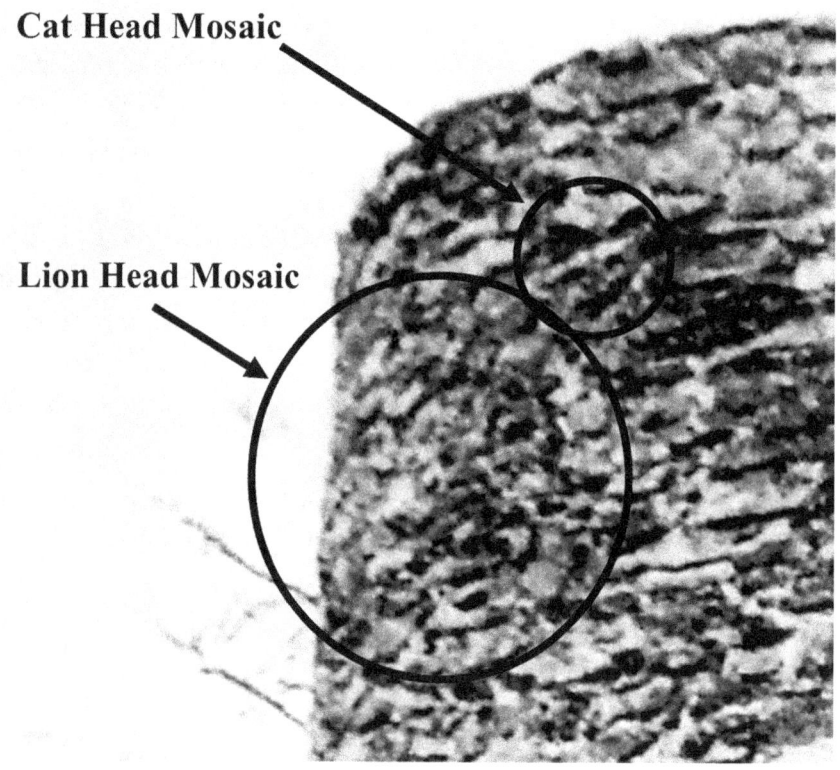

1895 photograph of Newport Tower showing lion head and cat head mosaics.
Source: Broader Britain: Published by The Werner Company of Chicago, 1895

He did not see anything at first, but as his eyes slowly adjusted, he did see a cat-like figure. "Yes, I do see it."

She slid her finger slowly across the photo then stopped near the top of the wall. "Do you see this white stone?" she asked. "I think it's deliberately positioned there. It seems out of place. All the stones that surround it are much darker." Mary began tracing an outline, using her finger. "It sort of looks like a helmet."

Maxwell followed her finger as she revealed a helmet, robe, feet, shoulders, and arms. There appeared to be a standing figure.

"My God," he whispered. "That looks like a knight." *All these years and theories, and no one has seen this?*

1895 photograph of Newport Tower showing
white-helmeted knight mosaic.
*Source: Broader Britain: Published by The Werner Company of
Chicago, 1895.*

"There is more," she said excitedly. "He is holding an object and—are you ready?—he appears to have a *cross on his chest!*"

Mary was so excited that she bolted out of her seat and started dancing around the room, her hair bouncing with every move.

Maxwell watched her in awe. He wanted to join her, but his nerves overtook him. He quickly walked over to the couch and sat down.

"Don't just sit there," Mary said, walking over to the computer and putting music on. Then she grabbed his hands and started to dance again.

He soon overcame his shyness and collided with her. It felt crazy, loose, and fun.

Mary danced closer and closer to him, using a cute sideways step. Then she threw her arms around him and kissed him, which took him by surprise, and he recoiled, although she didn't seem to notice.

"Can you see it?" she asked.

"Yes, I can," he answered. He couldn't believe his eyes or that such a beautiful woman had just kissed him.

After a few minutes of dancing, she said she had to go. Maxwell offered to drive her home again, but she graciously declined and called an Uber.

When the car arrived, she gave him another kiss on the cheek. Then, as she walked through the doorway, she turned toward him and gave a deadpan look. "Do not say a word about this to anyone. I have my reasons."

"I won't. I'll walk you out."

As they walked to the Uber, Mary told him about an assignment that she had once been given in her tenth-grade Spanish class that featured a rabbit hidden inside a picture. Mary had been the only student who could see the rabbit; her classmates could only see the obvious picture in front of them.

"You were the only one?" he asked.

"Yes," Mary said, appearing proud.

After saying their goodbyes, Maxwell walked back to the apartment building. At the door, he looked back to make sure

Mary was in the car. Then he walked inside, smiling to himself. The feeling about Mary was back.

As he was getting ready for bed, he glanced at the computer screen again and wondered how she could see things that others could not. He got into bed, turned on the television, and drifted into sleep.

***

The following day, the discoveries had still not sunk in. Maxwell kept staring at the computer screen as he was getting ready for class to confirm that his eyes had not been deceiving him the night before. The lion head, the cat head, and the knight still appeared to be there. Since their discovery, it was almost impossible to *un-see* them.

Later that day, he wanted to meet with Mary, so he called her to invite her to the Parrish Art Museum in Bridgehampton to discuss their finds and a plan.

Maxwell was extremely intrigued about the meaning of the discovery and how, when revealed, the archeological world would accept it. Since he had begun his studies, he had been determined to be a new type of archeologist who embraced and researched all finds and discoveries that were not the norm, that did not fit into history as written, and maybe even challenged it, with an open mind. He often thought that a world filled with turmoil and anger needed discoveries that injected unity from a higher place. Divisional findings needed to be reconnected, reevaluated, and reassessed through a different prism or perspective.

If the right artifact was found, or the right story was revealed, humanity could become unified around it. Maybe it was a dream, but he believed that a catalyst needed to be found soon, or humankind might perish in turmoil over the different religious ideologies and wars that had plagued the world's continents for thousands of years.

Maybe Newport Tower was that catalyst.

Chapter 3

MUSEUM

Maxwell parked at the Parrish Art Museum and met Mary near the entrance. They went in and walked to the crowded, little café. He moved a feeble metal table near a pair of chairs. The table scraped across the floor and made way too much noise for contemplating art. Embarrassed, he quickly sat down and looked around to see if anyone had noticed.

Mary had already positioned herself on a large windowsill nearby to take in the sunlight. Her profile was outlined in an expressed glow. She was radiant.

"How are you?" he asked.

"I am great. And you?"

"I'm wonderful."

"About last night ... with the kiss," Mary began. "I am so very sorry."

"There is no need to be," he said. "It was a fantastic night. I had a lot of fun."

Mary unfolded her arms. "I thought you would be a little taken aback."

"Nonsense. What are we going to do now?" he asked so that the painful conversation would end.

"How about we get some coffee?"

"Sure, sounds good."

Maxwell ordered from his phone then soon walked back to the table with two coffees.

"Have you been here before? I hear they have fantastic exhibits and special events," Mary said.

"No, I have driven by plenty of times on the way out east, though."

"After we finish our coffees, I am excited to view the galleries. What is your favorite style of art?" Mary asked.

"I am really drawn to impressionism. It is such a statement of artistic freedom. Imagine just painting a canvas and not worrying that you are not between the lines, so to speak. I once had an art teacher tell me that you could never mess up a painting and, you know, I believe him. What is art, anyway? Everyone's interests are so different."

"Interesting. I love impressionism, also," Mary said as she reached over and grabbed Maxwell's hand.

He looked down with surprise then nervously took a sip of his coffee.

"Tell me more about yourself, Maxwell."

"Well, I absolutely love peach tea."

They both laughed.

"I grew up on the east end of Long Island and still have family there. I worked from a young age in the family restaurant and, over time, the employees there grew to be my good friends and work family. I also spent a lot of time in nature, exploring the beach, following the Haul Seiners, fishing, clamming, catching crabs. I was a real Huckleberry Finn," Maxwell said, smiling, then continued.

"I lived in a windswept, forgettable place called Lazy Point. It was surrounded on three sides by water and filled with boyhood opportunities. My parents, brothers, and sisters all stayed in a tiny white house across from a pond filled with blue claw crabs. Looking back at it now, growing up there was magical.

Very different from today's hectic world. Have you ever picked a beach plum and made jam, or surf cast for bluefish?"

"No, I can't say that I have," Mary responded.

"I would like to take you one day, if that is okay with you?"

"That would be lovely."

They finished their coffees then walked in and out of the galleries, taking in the artwork, critiquing and commenting until Mary noticed a man who always seemed to be close by. He would stop a few yards away when they would stop and casually followed them into each gallery. He appeared to be interested in their conversation, glancing their way every so often.

"Maxwell, do you see that guy over there? Do you think he is following us?" Mary whispered.

"Maybe he thinks we're famous artists," Maxwell joked as he glanced at the man, who was wearing a well-fitted dark suit, his hair cut short. "I don't think he would be interested in two college students chatting in an art gallery."

"Especially peach tea drinkers," she said with a hint of a smile.

He wondered why Mary was so paranoid. Had something happened to her? She always seemed to be looking around, sometimes even past him when they spoke.

"I'll go stand next to him while pretending to look at a painting." Maxwell walked over to where the man stood, and the man backed up a few steps, turned, looked directly at Mary, ignoring him, and then left.

"Well, that was uncomfortable. Did you see him? He acted like I wasn't even there. He was staring at you. What a creep."

Mary appeared nervous.

Chapter 4

UNCLE

Maxwell arrived at his uncle's house in Southold—a well-built, 1970's ranch—and pulled into his driveway. His uncle would always boast about how his house had withstood Hurricanes Bob and Diane with minor damage, while often following up with, *"If it isn't broke, then leave it alone and live in it."*

Inside, the interior seemed to be timestamped. The carpet was orangish shag, and floral wallpaper adorned the walls, even in the kitchen. Vintage appliances were still in use, and polyester clothes were usually the staple. Maxwell had a theory that when people retired, they stopped going to stores to buy new items, especially clothes, unless they were oversized, dark sunglasses.

There was always a little mutt running around named Amerock. Maxwell thought the name was a complete misfit and suited for a much larger dog, like an Alaskan Malamute. The dog ruled the house.

Uncle was a proud man with sparse grey hair, hazel eyes, and a passion for art, history, and archeology. You could almost see his life chiseled in his face, wrinkle by wrinkle. Always popular at family picnics, he entertained guests with his tall tales of faraway places and odd characters whom he had met during his journeys.

He met Maxwell at the door, eager to hear the new finds briefly discussed with him when they had spoken on the phone earlier.

"How have you been?" Uncle asked as Amerock frantically sniffed his shoes.

"I'm great. Still going to school at Stony Brook and now working at the Museum of Natural History two days a week."

"When did you land that job?"

"Last November. I applied to the archeological department, and Dad knew someone, so I was able to secure a low-paying but interesting position."

"Great. What did you find?" Uncle never had much patience for small talk, and he always seemed like he was in deep thought or scatterbrained.

As Maxwell walked through the living room, he noticed artifacts and papers piled on every piece of furniture. He remembered an article that he had read once that clutter was a sign of brilliance. If so, his uncle was a genius.

In the kitchen, Maxwell's aunt was hovering over the sink. She had perfect brown hair and blue-green eyes. She always seemed to be in a sundress and apron, either cooking or cleaning. Upon hearing their footsteps, she turned around and reached out for a hug.

"Oh, Maxwell, you have grown into a fine young man!" she exclaimed. "Do you still take your coffee black?"

"Yes."

She had the memory of an elephant.

"I made your favorite—banana bread."

He heard his uncle fidgeting in the next room, probably trying to find something to show him.

"With all this crap around the house, it may take days," Aunt said in a serious tone. She did not have a love of discovery or collecting like Uncle. She tolerated his interests with love and seemed to ignore the mountains of stuff that grew larger each week.

"I try to keep his collections to one part of the house," she explained as she picked up a small quartz rock off the toaster oven.

"What are you collecting now, Uncle?" Maxwell yelled into the other room.

"Stamps, fine art, chairs, bottles, coins, dollar bills ... and *wives*," he quipped. He always had a dry sense of humor, often telling, laughing at, and commenting on his jokes. It was highly comical. Aunt did not always think so.

His aunt mouthed the word, "*chairs*," then shrugged in quiet defeat. "He did write a nice but strange story about chairs," she commented. She walked over to the dining room table that was covered with stacks of papers, in an attempt to find it, leaving only two places to eat. She looked around a bit then said, "Oh, never mind."

Uncle walked into the kitchen.

"Why do you collect chairs?" Maxwell asked.

"I plan on doing an exhibit of chairs through the ages. Think of all the nasty asses that sat in them." He bellowed a deep, rhythmic laugh that filled the room. Even Aunt laughed at that one.

"What the hell?" Maxwell whispered to his aunt, trying to subside his laughter.

"Have you ever read the book *America BC* by Dr. Barry Fell?" his uncle asked.

"No."

"Well, that is the book that really influenced me. I am trying to find my copy. Dr. Fell proves, through icons and linguistics, that the Egyptians were here in North America, hundreds of years before Columbus and even the Norse. He proves this by outlining the similarities between the Algonquian language and ancient Egyptian."

"That is fascinating," Maxwell said.

"What most people do not realize is that Dr. Fell found an inscribed tablet at Eagle Neck, in Orient on Long Island, not too far from here. It reads, '*This ship is a vessel from the Egyptian dominions.*' Dr. Fell theorized that early visitors from Egypt, during the Libyan Dynasty, could have traded with the Algonquians and taught them to use ideograms to express their stories in writing. This is a *bombshell*, Maxwell," Uncle said. "If you look at his analysis, there is little room for discount. Imagine how we could analyze the tablets today with new technology."

"Where are they now?" Maxwell asked.

"Reportedly lost … like all great, contradicting finds. Buried in untruths and bad logic. I, however, believe I found evidence that supports Dr. Fell's claim." Uncle's voice became a low whisper as he began looking around, as if expecting to see another person standing next to him. "What are you doing tomorrow?"

"I have a class in the morning, but after that, I'm free."

"Well, let's go out into the field, and I will show you. We have to be careful, though. The area is on someone else's property."

"Do you know them?"

"Oh, yeah … Well, kind of … I said hello in the post office once." Uncle laughed.

Maxwell could see the headline now: *College Student Arrested with Crazy Uncle Looking at Rocks, Trespassing.*

"I also found inscribed rocks with what appear to be petroglyphs. There are inscribed faces, also, on many of them. The history out here is intertwined and complex. The more we dig, the more we discover," Uncle said. "Are you hungry? Let's have some of your aunt's *world-famous* banana bread." He winked.

"Dear, could you bring us some of your world-famous banana bread?" he yelled into the kitchen where Aunt was ironing clothes.

Aunt walked out of the kitchen and proudly placed a large plate of banana bread down in front of Maxwell with a smile. It smelled great.

Maxwell took a bite and was sure to make *yum* noises as he chewed—not to appease her, but because it was delicious. With his mouth half-full, he let his aunt know that the banana bread was the best he had ever had and that she should enter it in the local agricultural fair.

Maxwell stayed an hour longer, talking and laughing about the old family reunions that they used to have on the family land near the Long Island Sound. Then he noticed that it was getting late and that his uncle was getting tired, so he excused himself and drove back to his apartment.

Chapter 5

POSSESSION IS EVERYTHING

Morning came quickly, and Maxwell was eager to meet up with his uncle to explore his claims.

When he knocked on his aunt and uncle's door, his uncle answered, dressed in a long white robe that had a large red cross along the chest.

"Good morning," he said.

"What's this?" Maxwell asked as Amerock danced around his feet, tail wagging.

"It is my fraternal robe."

Maxwell thought it was a little strange, but Uncle was not known for being ordinary.

"Would you like some coffee or tea?" Uncle asked as he slowly walked into the kitchen.

"Sure. Do you have any peach tea?" Maxwell stood in the kitchen doorway as he watched his uncle open a cabinet and reach in, noticing his aunt must not have been home.

Uncle spun around. "Who drinks peach tea? Not many men I know."

"Yeah," Maxwell said, cringing and taking a few steps backward. "Laurel recommended it. It's a new thing."

"Better be a new, *short* thing, for your sake."

"Regular tea is fine," Maxwell conceded.

Uncle grabbed a pea-green, vintage teapot off the stove and began to fill it with water. He placed it on the stove then gestured for them to walk to the dining room table and sit down. He grabbed a pipe from the middle of the table, filled it with tobacco, and lit it. Smoke billowed in a halo around his head as he tried to put the match out with a hand fan.

After a few minutes, Maxwell could hear the steam boil out of the kettle in a constant whistle. Uncle didn't move. Instead, he just sat there, staring at him, as if sizing him up to see if he was worthy.

Finally, Uncle began to speak, when someone knocked at the door.

"Can you go see who that is?" Uncle asked.

"Sure."

His uncle rose out of his chair and walked into the kitchen to turn off the stove and prepare the tea as Maxwell headed for the front door.

When Maxwell opened the door, he found a man standing there. A man who did not say a word.

Maxwell almost closed the door on him when the man walked past him, right into the house, and over to where his uncle who was now sitting.

"Maxwell, this is my uninvited friend, Joseph," Uncle introduced the man to Maxwell.

"Nice to meet you," Maxwell said.

Joseph looked to be in his early seventies. He had brown hair and vividly blue eyes.

"What are the two of you talking about?" Joseph asked oddly.

"Nothing," Uncle replied as Maxwell returned to his chair.

Joseph peered around the room, as if he were about to make a fantastic find.

The uncomfortable silence returned. After a few minutes, Joseph took the hint, headed for the door, and said he would call my uncle later to look at some rocks he had found.

"Maxwell, you have to be very careful," Uncle said quietly after Joseph had left. "As I started to say, the year was 2010, and I was exploring the farm fields and woodlands on the east end of Long Island and began to make discoveries that did not seem to fit in the claimed timeline of history. I found petroglyphs. One rock had a petroglyph that looked remarkably like a ship with several oars. I have a photo of it."

Uncle got up, walked over to the far side of the dining room, and then pulled out a colored photo of a rock from a drawer that squeaked when he opened it. He showed the picture to Maxwell. The boulder contained an image that did look remarkably like a ship and oars.

"This is an amazing find, Uncle," Maxwell said, holding up the photo.

Photograph of ship petroglyph, Southold, New York
M. B. Terry

"It makes sense that ancient people migrated here and survived with the bountiful natural resources," Uncle said. "On the east end of Long Island, there is everything they would have needed for thousands of years. This is evident from the number of artifacts that have been found and continue to be found. Are you aware that, during the 1930s and 1940s, amateur archeologists began to recover thousands upon thousands of artifacts from old Native American village sites now in the farm fields?"

"Where are the artifacts now?" Maxwell asked.

"They now sit in various collections in the American Museum of the Native American in New York City and the Southold Indian Museum. In Southampton, the Shinnecock tribe also maintains an excellent museum. They are the direct descendants of the early native populations."

His uncle continued, "The pursuit of land, materials, food, and life benefited peaceful times but also incited war throughout the ages. Peopled lived simply, but possession was everything. It was not much different in Ancient America than it is today. It was not by accident that the most critical records—deeds, transfers, observations—of one of the oldest English settlements in New York State were lost, never to be seen again."

"What happened to them?"

"No one knows. I think it was deliberately covered up or they buried the truth of what was discovered when the first colonists arrived. The early colonists wanted a new start, but they also wanted everything the Native Americans had. In their subtle suppression through religion and law, they eventually took it. The founding of America, in my opinion, was not only about religious freedom and survival, but was littered with opportunistic greed."

"Are we going in the field today to see the petroglyphs?" Maxwell asked.

"Not today. I tripped over a stack of books and hurt my hip. There will be no field trip today." Uncle ran his hand over his hip bone.

"I think they could have been inscribed by the Phoenicians, the Egyptians, the Romans, or the Knights Templar. All I know is that we are on the verge of great discoveries using new technology, such as Lidar—the imaging system that uses lasers to map objects.

"Many people just see what they are looking at in form—a pot is a pot, a rock is a rock—but for those who see, there is much more to these items. We have to look closer."

"Did you just say *for those who see*?"

"Yes. Why?"

"Nothing." Maxwell thought about the old book that Mary had shown him. She had said there had been a note that had once accompanied it. He thought the note said something similar but could not remember exactly what it was.

"I started this path of discovery, but I am getting older, and it will take a long time to convince the world," Uncle said. "We cannot ignore it, either! I wish we had an archeologist in the family when these items were being found."

"Soon enough, Uncle. I am going to start working on my thesis soon."

"What is the topic?"

"Well, I was thinking about trying to write about how the most expensive wood ever found was dug up on Oak Island. Do you watch the show *The Curse of Oak Island*?"

"You have that right." Uncle chuckled. "Yes, I love that show."

"No, seriously, I was going to do a study on the DNA of indigenous people of Long Island at a professor's suggestion, but now I may switch it to the origin of Newport Tower in Rhode Island."

His uncle leaned in. "Are you serious?"

"Yes. Why?"

"That tower has been studied over and over. There is much controversy and numerous theories behind the origin."

"So, you know about it?" Maxwell asked.

"Yes."

"My friend and I found some new evidence."

"I am listening."

"Well, we found some old photographs of the tower and anomalies in the rock structure. It turns out that the tower could be a mosaic."

"A mosaic about what?"

"We do not know yet. We found a figure of a lion's head, a cat's head, and a knight in the stonework."

"Hmm ..." Uncle leaned back in his chair. "I do not believe it."

"You don't believe it?" Maxwell exclaimed. "You, of all people, with all of your discoveries that no one can see but you, do not believe it? How ironic."

Uncle appeared insulted. He got up and slowly limped into the kitchen to place the empty tea mugs in the sink. "Let us talk this through again." Uncle limped over to the open curtains and closed them. Then he turned up the radio and reached for the newspaper on the table. As he began to speak, he crinkled up a page. "You can never be too careful," Uncle said as he looked around the room again.

"You know, when I first read of Newport Tower, I was fascinated with the theories of ancient origin and celestial alignments. I was so intrigued that I even have it on my list of places to visit. Who is your collaborator?" Uncle asked as he sat back down at the table.

"Her name is Mary. I met her in a local coffee house. You would not believe how beautiful she is. I mean, way out of my league."

"What does she look like?"

"She has deep blue eyes, long light-brown hair, and a lovely accent."

"An accent?" Uncle asked.

"Yes, she is British."

"I think I have some notes on the tower. I will give you a call when I find them."

Uncle stood up. "Well, it is time for you to go, Maxwell. I have to lay down and rest now. It has been great seeing you. Give my best to your dad."

Maxwell left his uncle's house and decided to call Mary on the way back to his apartment. Excited about the conversation, he mentioned that he had told his uncle about the lion, cat, and knight on the tower.

"What? Are you serious?" Mary shouted. "We agreed that you would not tell anyone. Bloody hell, Maxwell."

"I'm very sorry. My uncle is old and does not speak to many people." Maxwell knew this might not be the truth, but he also knew that his uncle was full of knowledge and explained to Mary that he might be able to help them.

After a few moments, Mary said, "Fine. I will forgive you this time, but please, let's keep this between us—and him—from now on. I will call you tomorrow." Mary ended the call.

Maxwell became filled with regret. He did not want their relationship to start this way. He decided that he would make it up to her and began thinking about how.

While parking his car, he became distracted and bumped into the car behind him. He looked in the rearview mirror and noticed a man sitting in the car, his dashboard dimly illuminating his face.

The man waved him off, so Maxwell exited his car and quickly entered his apartment. Inside, he kept the lights off and slightly pulled back a curtain to get a better look at the man, but the car was gone.

Chapter 6

THE ARK

Mary was troubled. What she was seeing was impossible. It did not make any sense, and she thought the world might not understand. She kept minimizing the window on her laptop computer, waiting a few minutes, and then opening it back up to look again. How had the photographer captured this in 1895? There were no computer manipulations or doctoring of photos in those times. She only hoped that Maxwell would be able to see it, too.

After hours of staring at the image, she needed a break, so she put the laptop down. Nevertheless, her mind was racing, trying to process something that just should not be there. She thought she was going mad or had developed some condition where you saw things that weren't there.

She reached for her computer again and began to type. She figured she had come this far and must write down what she had seen and maybe, just maybe, reveal it to the world someday.

Let the archeological community argue whether the figures are there or not, she thought. *I have to try to explain this.*

She started to type:

What I see here is challenging to explain. However, I will try to discuss it here.

The photograph of the south window, taken in 1895 by an unknown photographer, is extraordinarily complex. What the photographer captures is, on all levels, illogical. When I zoom into the south window image and to the back wall, I see what appears to be a box-like container, oriented from left to right. Interestingly, the box seems to have one dark triangle on the left side that forms a handle. The right handle is obscured. Strikingly, there appears to be a straight line near the top of the box that extends from left to right and looks like a representation of a top or lid. Finally, there appears to be three dark figures hovering just above the box with distinctive headdresses. I have included the figure below.

However, what is most extraordinary is that there appear to be three or four vertical lines topped with small circles and points that seem to form the shape of a crown in the foreground, which partially obscures the box. The crown sits on a skull-like figure facing left and holding a staff with a cross to the left (not the white line running over the photo through the window). A second face is facing right with a long, pointed nose. Yes, there appear to be two figures in the foreground of the box—one facing left and one right. The figure(s) also seem to be flanked by what appears to be additional figures on each side. Below, I have separated the two faces with a white line in the photo.

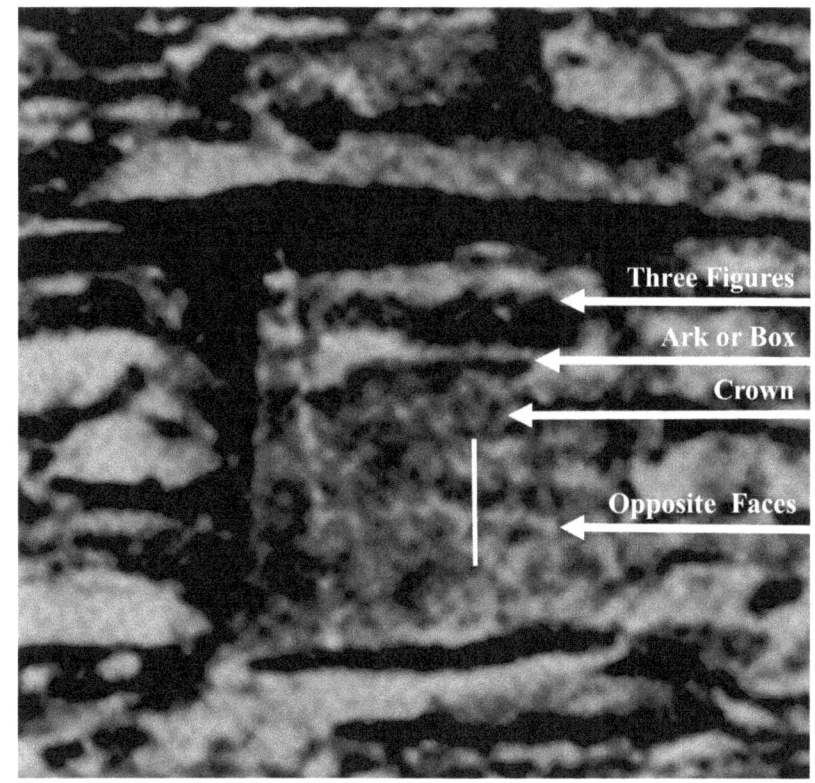

1895 photograph of Newport Tower south window,
showing: ark, crown and two opposite, facing faces.
Source: Broader Britain: Published by The Werner Company of Chicago, 1895.

Mary slammed the laptop shut, stood up, and began pacing around the room. *This is absurd*, she thought.

Heartbeat quickened, she sat down again and started petting her cat, Matt, who was curled up in the corner of the couch. The cat began to purr, and Mary could feel herself calming down. It had been an excellent choice to name the cat after Matthew the Apostle, her mother's favorite saint. The cat worked wonders.

This is bloody madness. What am I seeing? Mary thought to herself again. *Who in their right bloody mind is going to believe this?*

She began to type again.

> It may make sense that the tower would be decorated with figures and even symbols claiming ownership and purpose; however, the photo's details cannot be given a rational explanation. Historians claim that the tower was once covered in a stucco material, and maybe this material formed these shapes and has since eroded.

Mary did not know what to do now. She was beginning to believe more and more that this structure might be of worldwide religious significance.

"Sorry, Benedict Arnold, but this structure is certainly not a bloody mill," she said out loud. "What do you think, Matt?"

Mary decided to try again to take a break. Her body was tired, but her brain was wide awake, firing thoughts in several directions at once. She brushed her teeth and got into bed. Hours passed, and all she did was toss and turn. She wanted to call Maxwell, but when she looked at the clock on her nightstand, she saw that it was one a.m. and too late. She tried to divert her thinking to walking through fields of flowers in her homeland and picnics with her mum and dad, but nothing worked. Finally, her thoughts began to fade, and she felt herself drifting off to sleep.

***

The following day, as she began brushing her teeth, she glanced into the mirror with her toothbrush sticking out of the side of her mouth and noticed Matt staring at her from the couch.

"I am not crazy ... The lion's head, the cat, and the knight are distinct and not refutable, but these figures are extraordinary.

How can they even exist? I know, I know ... You're a cat. Are you hungry?"

She got dressed then walked into the kitchen to feed the cat. "Tomorrow, I will go to the library to see if other structures were decorated with similar symbols ... Mary, you must be quite out of your mind," she said softly.

***

Mary perused the stacks at the library and stopped at a large book titled *Knights Templar Encyclopedia* by Dr. Karen Ralls. She flipped through it.

Dr. Ralls talked about the history of the guild, an association of craftsmen, or merchants, formed in Medieval Times for mutual aid and protection, and to further their professional interests. The Medieval guilds were of two types—the merchant and the craft guild.

Craft guild? Mary thought. *Are the complicated symbols on Newport Tower made by such craftsmen? That could be it.*

This demanded much more investigation and research, but she ran out of time and had to go to class. Mary packed up her things. She was nervous and excited to meet Maxwell after class at the coffee shop.

***

Maxwell was already at the busy coffee shop when Mary arrived. She ran into a friend of hers, and they hugged and walked together toward the serving counter. Maxwell watched from his familiar, overstuffed chair as the two women chatted. Mary was talking animatedly with her hands, as if she were explaining a story.

Maxwell tried not to feel left out when Mary brought two steaming cups of tea to his table and set them down next to him. He pretended to be engrossed with his reading.

"That was my friend, Asha," Mary said. "She is from India. This is her first time in America, and she is quite excited. At the beginning of the school year, I met her at a social. I told her that we should meet up soon."

"Sounds nice," Maxwell said, even though he was not explicitly being asked to go.

"She has a boyfriend named Amritsar. She calls him Amri. Isn't that cute? Maybe we can all go together."

"Great," Maxwell said as he sunk deeper into the chair. "So, what did you want to tell me?"

Mary did not want to talk about the discovery that she had made about the box in the south window now. She had never felt the coffee shop was a safe place for confidential conversations.

She knew it would be exceedingly difficult to understand, and after she thought about it for a while, she needed a lot more time to process the discoveries herself. She also did not want Maxwell to become confused, and she had a real fear of no one else even seeing the images. She was beginning to think they were not even there. However, she did believe that the lion, cat, and knight were enough to investigate and take a trip to Newport.

"I think we should try to go to Newport Tower to see if the lion, cat, and knight we saw on the computer are still there. They are discoveries that the world needs to see someday."

Mary waited for Maxwell to answer. She had noticed that he was sometimes slow to respond because he was a thinker.

"I like that idea. We could try to recreate the photo in the field."

"Yes. And, do you know that the winter solstice is coming up? I read somewhere that the tower is celestially aligned."

"With what?"

"I can't remember, but it would be exciting to find out."

"So, we agree that we are going to go?" he asked.

"Yes."

Asha waved from across the room as she sipped her coffee, and Mary gestured for her to come over to where she and Maxwell sat.

"Asha, this is Maxwell, my friend," Mary said when Asha arrived.

Maxwell stood up and extended his hand to shake Asha's.

All Mary could think about was how she had just introduced him as a *friend*, not a *boyfriend*. She glanced at Maxwell and smiled, hoping he was not offended.

"I was thinking," Mary said to Asha. "Would you and Amri be open to having drinks with Maxwell and me sometime?"

"Sure," Asha replied.

"Great. How about this Saturday night? That is good for you, right, Maxwell?"

"Yes," Maxwell said.

"I will check with Amri, but that should be good," Asha said.

Mary stood up, hugged Asha, and said goodbye. Then she sat back down.

"I decided to go to the library and research Medieval architecture," Mary said after Asha had left. "I found some great information on Medieval craft guilds that I wanted to tell you about. I wrote some information down."

Mary reached into her backpack and pulled out a notebook. She then opened it and pointed to her notes. "You see, here it says that Medieval guilds were associations of artisans and craftsmen, like weavers, bookbinders, masons, and architects in the building trade—painters, metalworkers, etcetera—and that the Medieval craft guilds became widespread in the eleventh century in Europe. Did you know that the word *craft* comes from the old English word meaning *skill*?"

"No, I did not. How interesting."

Maxwell watched a battle between a baby and mom across the room as Mary spoke.

"We can leave during winter break, and that would put us in Newport during the winter solstice," Mary said excitingly.

"Good, winter ..." Maxwell said distractedly.

The baby kept throwing her pacifier on the floor and laughing, and the mom kept picking it up. This occurred five times before the mom grew tired of the game and took away the pacifier.

His mind shifted to the trip. Would they book two hotel rooms as friends, or one as a couple? Was she going to sleep alone or with him?

The mom handed the baby the pacifier again, and the baby threw it on the floor again, giggling. *If we could all be entertained so simply*, he thought.

"I mean, that is a fantastic idea," he said without looking at her. "We can take my car."

"Is something wrong, Maxwell?"

"No, not at all. Are we booking one hotel room, or two? I would like to stay where my family stayed when we went to Newport when I was a boy—The Inn at Castle Hill. I will pay for it."

Mary was unfamiliar with the place but agreed. "Are you sure you want to pay for the room?"

"Should I book one room or two rooms?" Maxwell asked again.

Mary looked at him quizzically. "One room, silly."

Maxwell perked up. "When I get home, I will make the reservations. Right now, let's just sit here and enjoy the moment." He took a sip of his tea.

Mary started reading a book that she had pulled out of her backpack, and Maxwell watched the mother and baby pack up to leave.

Mary reached over and softly held Maxwell's hand.

Chapter 7

THE VISIT

On a cold, December morning, one day before the winter solstice, Mary and Maxwell left Stony Brook to catch an early Orient-New London Ferry to Newport, Rhode Island. On the way, Maxwell was nervous and stressed about the sleeping arrangements, but he did not know how to ask her about them. After a while, he realized he was overthinking it, so he forced himself to focus on the discoveries.

"Mary, I want you to know that the last few weeks I have spent with you have been the best in my life."

"How sweet of you to say that. Corny, but sweet," she said as they both laughed. "Where is your family from? I mean, when did they arrive in America?"

"They were the first to arrive at Southold on the east end in 1640."

"I am from Southwold, and you are from Southold ... I wonder if there is a connection. Where did your family emigrate from?"

"Well, you are not going to believe this, but I can't remember. Let's call my uncle." Maxwell prompted his car's speakerphone to dial his uncle's number.

"Hello?" his uncle answered. "Quit bothering me, you cold-calling scumbags. If I wanted to buy your shitty vacation package, I would call you ... And another thing, my accounts have not been hacked, and you cannot have my social security number, you annoying losers. I am going to report you to ... to ... to *someone*. Next time you idiots call, the only thing you're going to hear is an air horn."

Embarrassed, Maxwell turned to Mary, who was trying to control her laughter.

"Uncle, Uncle, it's me, Maxwell."

His uncle's tone changed immediately. "Oh, Maxwell, how are you? Did you get married to that girl yet?"

Maxwell frantically pressed buttons on the steering wheel, trying to take his uncle off speakerphone, but he couldn't find the right one.

"I have a question," he said quickly before his uncle could say anything else. "Where did our family originate from?"

"What do you mean?"

"Where did we sail from to arrive in America?"

"Oh, Long Sutton, England."

"Okay, thank you. I may stop by in a few weeks. We are heading to Newport now."

"Great. Let me know what you—"

Maxwell pressed the *end-call* button to avoid any further embarrassment.

"You told him about me?" Mary asked.

"Yes, something I may regret. And, to answer your second question, I have five brothers and two sisters."

"That is a big family. I am the only child in mine," Mary said.

They spent the next hour and a half engaged in small talk, reaching The Inn at Castle Hill just before noon.

Maxwell pulled the car to the front of The Inn and went inside to check in. The lobby was a cozy room with dark wood walls. A man sat in a chair, reading a newspaper beside a fireplace that warmed the space with a flickering glow. A small bar was off to the side.

An attendant was busy at the front desk, and as Maxwell waited to get his attention, he looked back to check on Mary. She had gotten out of the car and was stretching her legs. The cold breeze off the sea blew her hair around.

"May I help you?" the attendant finally asked, looking up at Maxwell.

"Yes, I have a reservation."

"Your name?"

"Maxwell Downs."

"Yes, I see here that you have a reservation for one room with a king bed."

"Is it possible to upgrade to a suite?" Maxwell asked.

"Normally, we're busy this time of year, but with the big storm coming—they're forecasting ten inches of snow, an Alberta Clipper that will be out of here by morning—we have many rooms available." The attendant pushed a few buttons then scanned his screen. "I can put you in the Lighthouse Suite on the third floor."

"Sure, that would be excellent," Maxwell replied.

Maxwell finished checking in then returned to the car.

"Okay, we are good. I was able to upgrade to a suite with a king bed and a pull-out couch. They said there is a storm coming, and they have many vacancies."

"A storm?" Mary asked.

"Yes, they are expecting around ten inches of snow. Good for us because the restaurants and park will not be crowded."

They walked up to the third floor, where Maxwell swung open the door to their room, propping it with his foot to allow Mary to enter first.

She gasped. "Maxwell, this is gorgeous. How did you even afford it?"

"It is called the Lighthouse Suite," he said, intentionally evading the question.

Mary walked around the room, touching the surfaces of the furniture with approval and admiring the nautical-themed photos on the wall behind the couch.

Maxwell checked out the bathroom. "Bathroom is very nice!" he called.

When he came back into the main room, he noticed a bottle of wine and two glasses on a small table near the window.

Mary smiled.

"Let's go into Newport and grab a bite to eat," Maxwell said.

As they walked down the hotel staircase, Mary said she was in the mood for good fish and chips, like she used to have back home in Southwold. On the way, they decided to pass Touro Park and see the tower as they drove.

"There it is!" Maxwell exclaimed.

The tower was majestic, and just how it looked in the photo —made of stones and surrounded by an iron fence painted black. The grey-cloud-filled sky framed it perfectly.

What a lovely park, Maxwell thought. He noticed how it formed a central space surrounded by churches and historic homes. Several benches, statues, and trees were scattered about, and a woman walked her dog down one of the paths.

"Yes, I am so excited to come back for the solstice tomorrow," Mary said as she clapped her hands. "I checked TripAdvisor while you were in the lobby, and it recommends the Brick Alley Pub for fish and chips. It is right in the middle of town, on Thames Street."

"Sounds good. Let's try it, and then we can walk around," Maxwell said.

Snow began to fall as Maxwell and Mary entered the Brick Alley Pub and waited for the hostess to seat them. It was a busy place with art on the walls, dark tables, a central bar, and a nice salad bar. The place was alive with motion and chatter.

Maxwell wondered how many of the customers had heard of the tower, or would even care once their secret was revealed.

They were quickly seated, and a young girl approached them. "Hi, my name is Morgan. It's my first night," the waitress said with a thick New England accent.

"Don't worry; we're easy," Mary told her. "I used to wait tables, so I know how it is. How are the fish and chips?"

"They are wicked good," the waitress replied.

Mary ordered a root beer and the fish and chips while Maxwell flipped the menu back and forth, trying to make up his mind.

"Maxwell," Mary said, motioning to the waitress, who appeared to be in a hurry.

Finally, he chose a local craft beer and the French dip.

They handed the menus back to the waitress then waited for their drinks. Mary was quiet and seemed a little lost in thought.

When the drinks arrived, Maxwell asked, "What are you thinking?" He took a sip of his beer. "Wow, that is bitter." He placed it on the table.

"Oh, I thought that we have come so far, so fast, and if I had not met you in the coffee shop, none of this would have ever happened." Mary took a sip of her root beer then casually placed her hand on the table near the fork.

Maxwell began to move his hand to meet hers, sensing she needed comfort, when the waitress interrupted them.

"French dip?" she said, standing above the table, holding their plates.

"Here." Maxwell gestured to the space in front of him.

"Here you go." The waitress placed the fish and chips in front of Mary.

"This looks amazing!" Maxwell complimented.

"Do you need anything else?" the waitress asked.

"No, thank you," Maxwell answered.

Mary looked up and smiled.

After they finished eating, Maxwell suggested they walk to a cupcake place that he had noticed down the street. On the way, a mother with a little girl passed. The girl had a grin on her face as she held up a cupcake, as if to show him.

Inside the cupcake store, Maxwell grabbed Mary's hand as they took their place in line. The girls behind the counter were busily grabbing and packing cupcakes.

Once they arrived at the counter, Mary's eyes grew wide as she peered into the glass case, at the many cupcakes arranged in neat rows. "Do you want to share a peanut butter and chocolate one?" she asked.

"Sure."

"We will have a peanut butter chocolate cupcake, please," she requested.

The girl behind the counter grabbed, packed, and handed Mary a cupcake that dripped with chocolate and peanut butter drizzle. Maxwell immediately reached over and grabbed napkins.

They continued walking throughout downtown, looking in store windows as the snow fell, stopping to take bites here and there until Maxwell noticed that Mary seemed cold.

"Would you like to go back to The Inn?" he asked.

"Yes," Mary replied.

They walked back to the car then drove to The Inn, passing the tower, which was now lit up and looked majestic in the falling snow and evening light.

As they walked through the lobby, the desk clerk called out to Maxwell, "Mr. Downs, a man was looking for you and asking questions about you and the lady. Specifically, if you were staying here."

Maxwell stopped walking. "Wait—what?"

"Yes, an older man was looking for you about two hours ago. I told him that it was company policy never to give out information about who is or is not our guest. He left quickly."

"Thank you, sir," Maxwell said then he and Mary continued walking.

"What do you think that was about?"

"I have no idea. Who would know we are here?" Mary questioned.

Inside their room, Mary quickly drew the curtains closed, peered out into the fading light, and then sat down on the couch. She pulled out the novel that she had been reading. Maxwell thought she was trying not to reveal her nervousness about the unexpected visitor.

"How about a glass of wine?" he asked.

"Sure, sounds lovely."

Maxwell walked over to where the wine and glasses were and poured two glasses. He relaxed, turning on the television to watch the weather. He hoped that the snow would stop and the skies would clear before the solstice.

"How would you like to sleep?" He was finding it difficult to concentrate, growing nervous about the sleeping arrangements and did not want to be presumptuous.

Mary stopped reading and put her hand on his thigh. "I think we should sleep together, but I want to take it slow with us."

Maxwell was relieved. He thought it was a small victory that they would sleep in the same bed. Who knew what the night might have in store?

Mary prepared for bed then got in. She moved closer to Maxwell, who put his arm around her. They both slept peacefully through the night.

***

Maxwell got up a few hours before dawn and woke Mary.

"It's time to get up. We have to get to the tower before sunrise."

While Mary stirred, Maxwell exited the room to grab coffees in the lobby. Mary was dressed and ready to go when he returned.

They drove to the tower, and as they neared, his excitement grew. Maxwell parked the car and could see a large crowd gathered on the west and south sides of the tower. It was freezing, so Maxwell cuddled Mary, taking her hands into his to warm them as they walked to find a good spot to watch the sunrise. They all seemed to be standing there, waiting for the precise moment ... everyone except a cowering old man with a walking stick. He approached the crowd from the eastern path with a slow, deliberate gait.

Maxwell was bursting with anticipation. Mary stood to his right, shivering.

"It is so cold," she complained, putting her hands in his pockets.

"A few more minutes," he said, trying to comfort her.

People were huddled together in little groups. Maxwell overheard someone say that they had driven from Denver, Colorado just for this event.

The cowering old man kept slowly approaching and stopped at each group of people, making his rounds around the tower. He drew closer and closer to where Maxwell and Mary stood.

Maxwell noticed how he would stop at each couple or group of people and ask them a question. They would shake their heads to signal an exaggerated *no* in the pre-dawn light.

The old man looked out of place. He wore a long, white cloak that dragged in the snow under a long, black overcoat. *Maybe he's a priest, blessing everyone*, Maxwell thought.

He scanned the crowd to see if anyone else was dressed in such a manner. One other odd fellow leaned against a large oak tree north of the tower, his face obscured by the shadows.

At that moment, a cold chill went up Maxwell's spine. He reached into his pocket to grab Mary's hand—her hands were freezing. Then he pulled her close so that he could whisper to her, "Do you see that man over there near that tree in the shadows?"

Mary started looking in all the wrong places.

"To our right, near the other tree," Maxwell clarified.

"Yes," she replied.

"He has been looking in this direction for some time. I think he is looking at us. Do me a favor and walk away from me, and I will see if his head follows you."

"Okay." Mary began to walk to the south side of the tower. Sure enough, the man in the shadows readjusted his stance and angle. Mary seemed to notice, as well, and quickly returned to Maxwell.

Nearby, a tall man approached the tower with a small group following closely behind. Maxwell overhead him say he was the director of something as he highlighted different stones and windows on the tower with a green laser pointer.

"The tower was once covered in a stucco-type material," the man said as he pointed the laser to the areas of remaining stucco. He then pointed to a header above one of the windows. "The header of this window is made of stone—"

"What is a header?" a little girl bundled in heavy clothes interrupted him. She was having difficulty walking, and all Maxwell could see was her round face. Her hat and mittens were adorned with lions.

"A header is the top of a window," the man answered.

"Oh," she responded as she shuffled closer to the man.

The man then pointed to a light beige stone with two notches at the top and explained it was a significant stone in the structure and that some believed it to be a keystone.

"What is a keystone?" the little girl asked.

"A keystone is an important stone in buildings."

"Oh," the little girl said as she tried to walk in step with him.

"If you look through this window, there is an egg-shaped stone that some people think represents Venus," the man continued. His green laser light landed on a stone shaped like an egg.

The little girl looked up quizzically and asked, "Who is Venus?"

"It is not a *who*, dear. It is a planet," the tall man explained. "This stone may represent the planet, Venus. It is still under debate."

"No, isn't she a tennis player, Mommy?" the little girl asked as she turned toward the woman standing behind her.

The tall man paused, took a deep breath, and then looked impatiently toward the sky. The little girl did, too.

"What is up there?" she asked.

By this time, the group was highly entertained and laughed every time she spoke. She was making the cold wait more bearable.

The tall man waited for the next question as he began to move to a new location. His pace quickened, and the little girl tried her best to keep up as he rounded the tower.

He stopped and spoke directly to the little girl. "Venus is a planet in our solar system that is very important to people in history and today."

Maxwell thought the man was trying to use words that the girl would understand.

"It is a planet with sacred meanings and symbolism."

"And a tennis player," the little girl said proudly.

The man looked down at her. "Yes, and a tennis player."

With that explanation, the tall man moved even more quickly, like he was trying to distance himself from the little girl.

Maxwell watched the episode unfold and thought that the little girl was adorable. He wondered how many people would be interested in Mary's lion, cat, and knight discovery if they seemed to be so interested in window headers. He began to look more closely at the headers of the windows. *I wonder if those stones could be inscribed?*

The tall man went on to discuss an elaborate theory from a fellow named John Dee. He delved into how the tower had been discovered to be positioned to astrological alignments. He was a wealth of information, and Maxwell found him knowledgeable and intriguing.

Suddenly, the crowd grew quiet as the sunlight began to break the horizon and ascend toward the west window. The tall man was narrating the events as they happened.

"In time, the sun will shine through the west window, illuminating the inside of the tower and eventually shine on the egg-shaped, or Venus, stone. It will pierce the darkness as it has done for thousands of years in this very spot."

Maxwell began to walk around the tower to get a better view. It was difficult to maneuver because the crowd had grown larger and more dense. He found the best spot he could, looked up, and waited.

Over his right shoulder, someone whispered, "Do you see it?"

"What?" Maxwell asked, not wanting to look behind him for fear of missing the exact moment when the sunlight would illuminate the stone.

"The holiness of this structure?"

"Yes," Maxwell said, not knowing how to answer. "Tell me more," he added, hoping to appease this person.

There was a period of silence as the sun began to creep closer to the egg-shaped stone. The light seemed more intense than usual, as if the sunrays were concentrated.

As the light spread through the window, it illuminated the stone perfectly. The crowd cheered and clapped. Maxwell was impressed and turned to look at Mary, but she was gone.

He heard the voice behind him again.

"This tower is ancient."

Who the hell is this? Maxwell thought, and as he spun around, he realized it was the man with the walking stick who had approached the other groups earlier. His face was chiseled with age lines, crow's feet, and a permanent frown. He wore a large silver cross around his neck, outside of his black overcoat.

The man reached out and grabbed Maxwell's arm at the elbow. Maxwell jerked from his grip just after the man shoved a small piece of paper into his hand. He then turned and quickly walked away.

"What the hell is this?" Maxwell whispered.

He went to find Mary, who was standing on the south side of the tower.

"You will not believe what just happened. This old man claimed this tower is holy, grabbed me by the elbow, and shoved this piece of paper into my hand." He opened his fist to reveal the paper. "What do you think that was about?"

"I don't know, but you should sterilize that hand," Mary said, taking the paper and beginning to read.

For those who see ...
Meet Dr. Cornelius Strum at the Salve Regina
University, Ochre Court, at 12:12 p.m. tomorrow.

Mary's face brightened as she read, and her eyes grew wide.

"What?" Maxwell asked. The sun was higher, and he could feel its warmth interrupting the cold.

"It says, '*For those who see …*' and that he wants us to meet a Dr. Strum tomorrow at Salve Regina University. What does that mean? And, why is this place so strange?"

"Why me?" Maxwell asked. "Why would some random old man come up and speak to *me*?"

"I don't know," Mary said, shaking her head.

"He could be nuts," Maxwell said, trying to downplay the experience.

Mary looked unconvinced as the sun broke from behind the tower and illuminated the paper in her hand. The paper looked ancient, as it was yellow and brittle.

"It looks like it was written on papyrus," Mary noted.

"Papyrus? No way."

Mary turned the paper over in her hands, revealing three faint crosses on the back side.

Behind Mary, two people were in a heated argument. Their breath vapors filled the air around them as they spoke. One claimed that The Order of Christ from Portugal had been the builder of Newport Tower.

Maxwell's focus shifted to finding the old man again. He scanned the crowd, which was dispersing in all directions. In the distance, he caught a glimpse of him and grabbed Mary's hand. "Come on," he whispered as he began to jog after the man.

Mary dropped his hand and did not follow. "No, Maxwell, it may be too dangerous."

Maxwell agreed and walked back to where Mary stood. Behind her, the sun continued creeping over the stones. Then he pointed. "Hey, do you see them?"

"I can't believe it, but yes, they are still here." She pointed to the location of the lion. "There is the lion and the cat. They are not as prominent or distinct in this light as the photograph, but they are *here*!" she said excitedly. She then pointed to the white rock that capped the knight. "And here is the knight." She traced the outline in the air.

All Maxwell could do was mutter, "Wow, this is unbelievable. This is surely not a mill, as some historians have claimed for hundreds of years."

Mary spent more time looking at the south window as Maxwell took many photographs of the tower from all directions. By now, it was mid-morning.

Maxwell could see Mary trying to gain a better perspective of the tower. She walked back and forth, closer and farther away, as if searching for something.

He saw her stop as if what she had been looking for had been found. Then she walked back to Maxwell. "Can you take some photos of this window?"

"Sure," Maxwell replied.

1895 photograph of south view of Newport Tower showing, lion head, cat head and knight mosaics.
Source: Broader Britain: Published by the Werner Company of Chicago, 1895.

***

On the way back to the hotel, Mary went on and on about the old man in the park and the piece of paper. Maxwell could not remember where she had been standing during the solstice. He had lost sight of her when he had moved to the window to get a better vantage point.

"I touched the tower."

"How did you do that?" he asked.

"Well, the tall man with the green thingamajig opened the gate, and while he was explaining stones and features, I was able to put my hand on it."

"That's probably illegal," he said. "But neat."

Back at the hotel, Maxwell sat down at the desk and wrote down what had occurred at the tower. He had more questions than answers.

"I am going to look at the tower photos again," Mary said, pulling out her laptop. "I have this feeling that there is a lot more to it than what we have discovered so far."

"You do?" Maxwell responded. He walked over to where Mary was sitting and pulled out his phone to search for the new photos of the tower.

"Here is a photo of a different section of the tower. Do you see anything?" He held up the phone for Mary to see.

"I think it is too difficult on such a small screen. Will you email it to me?"

Mary started humming a song.

"What is that song? It is very beautiful," Maxwell wondered.

"Oh, I did not realize I was humming it. My mum used to sing it to me when I was young."

"I like it," Maxwell said.

They researched the tower until evening but did not find anything further.

"Do you want to go to dinner soon? I found a vegetarian café that I think you would enjoy."

"Sounds brilliant."

***

The dinner conversation started slow as they tried to take in all of the day's events.

Finally, Mary asked, "Do you think we should meet him? Dr. Strum?"

"I don't know. This has gotten way too weird. I mean, out of all the people there, why did the old man give the note to us? Was he the old man who came to The Inn?"

"Who else knows we are here and what we discovered?" Mary asked.

"As I said, I only told my uncle, but he would not tell anyone. He lives in his own world, somewhere between reality and crazy." Maxwell cracked a smile, hoping to lighten the mood, but Mary remained serious. "Did you tell anyone?"

"No," she replied as she took a sip of her beer.

"Salve Regina University is not far from here," Maxwell said. "I think it is in the Mansion District. Since it's a school, there will be many people around. We should be safe. Why don't we meet him tomorrow, and after meeting with him, we can take a walk on the Cliff Walk past the mansions, if it is warm enough? You seem a little aggravated. It may help clear your mind."

"I am aggravated, but just a little. Something I saw in a photo was not on the tower in real life ... I wanted to validate it before I showed you, but I could not find it."

"Oh?"

Mary looked down at her plate.

"Are you going to eat your potato?" he asked.

"No, you can have it."

"Great. I love baked potatoes. You do know that Long Island was once known for their potatoes?"

"No, I did not."

"What is Southwold known for?" Maxwell asked.

"A brewery, pier, lighthouse, inns, and a beach ... much more exciting than a potato." Mary giggled. "It has these quaint, multicolor beach huts. My dad used to rent one, and we used to buy fish and chips at this little place called—you guessed it —the Little Fish and Chip Shop on East Street. I long for those days again when I was a little girl. I am exhausted. Let's head back to The Inn."

"Sounds like a good idea."

They finished dinner then left the café.

When they entered their hotel room, Maxwell finally felt tired after the long day. Mary said she wanted to shower, and as he heard the running water, he felt himself falling asleep, unaware that someone was watching him outside the hotel window.

Chapter 8

MEETING

"I am a little nervous about this meeting," Mary said the next morning.

"We will be fine," Maxwell reassured her.

They drove to Salve Regina University where they reported to the security office. They found a campus map at the kiosk then proceeded to the Ochre Court building. As they approached, they could see a man with gray hair leaning against a column near the entrance.

"Are you Dr. Strum?" Mary asked.

"Yes, I am." He extended his hand. "Let's go to my office," he said as he began to walk away quickly. Maxwell and Mary followed.

They entered his office cautiously, and as the door was swung open, they could see a space crowded with old furniture, rocks, artifacts, and piles of paper tucked in areas one would not expect. The smell of old, musty, decaying paper filled the air, and there was no place to sit down, nor hardly a place to write on the desk. The office reminded Maxwell of his uncle's house.

"Sorry for the mess," Dr. Strum apologized. "I am a researcher."

Mary asked if he could crack the window open. And, as Dr. Strum raised the blinds, beams of sunlight spotlighted dust dancing around the room.

Mary walked over to an old telescope that was stored in the corner. It was surrounded by various stones of all shapes, sizes, and colors. Stepping over them and a few piles of papers, she reached out her hand.

"Do not touch that!" Dr. Strum exclaimed. "That is an achromatic reflector telescope made by Henry Fitz Jr. on Long Island. He was a pioneer in astronomy and photography. It is very old and fragile."

Mary refocused on Dr. Strum when she heard the words *Long Island.*

As Strum continued speaking, she looked around the room. The walls were filled with diplomas and various awards, but one small, oak frame hanging above the telescope caught her eye. It was an old, browning piece of paper with the words "*For Those Who See*" handwritten in English and Latin.

Mary's and Maxwell's eyes met.

"Um ... Dr. Strum, was it you who handed Maxwell the piece of paper at the park? And, can I ask where you got that oak wood frame?" Mary asked.

"No, it was one of my colleagues. And, what wood frame?" he quickly moved on.

"The one that says, '*For those who see*,'" she said.

Dr. Strum stood up from his desk, walked over to the frame, and stared at it for a good minute. "I do not know. I think I bought it at a flea market in Bristol."

Mary remembered her grandfather's book and the letter. Inscribed was the same saying. But he lived in the United Kingdom, and this was hanging on a wall in the United States. At the tower, someone had also whispered the words behind Maxwell.

How odd, she thought. Things were becoming strange, but as her father had taught her, you should be direct if something was bothering you and you were not in danger.

Before she could ask, Dr. Strum started firing off questions at Mary.

"Where are you from? What was your mother's name? How did you two meet?"

"We just met, and I will not answer those other questions," she replied sternly and took a few steps back toward the door. His questions were invasive and rude. "Why are we here?"

"I am investigating for a book that I am writing about people's attraction of the tower through the centuries, so I had one of my colleagues randomly hand out invitations for interviews at the park."

That's rubbish, Mary thought.

"What does the phrase in that oak frame mean?"

"No idea, but it was one of my best flea markets buys to date. May bring it to the *Antiques Roadshow*," he said with a low chuckle.

Mary was not buying it. She did not reply or ask a follow-up question. She just stared at Dr. Strum.

As the minutes passed, Dr. Strum seemed to grow uncomfortable. He excused himself to use the restroom.

"I think this guy is really off, Maxwell."

"I agree. Let's give him some more time and see what else he has to say. I mean, he is kind of interesting."

"One more personal question about me, and we are out of here," Mary said.

A few more minutes passed, and Mary decided to check the hallway. As she looked left, she could see a man's silhouette at the end, pacing nervously back and forth in front of a window. Mary returned to Maxwell and told him what she had seen.

After a few more minutes, Dr. Strum returned, sat down, and took a deep breath. "Well, that phrase is from an ancient order of protectors who were so secret that even their family members did not know about it," he finally admitted.

"Like the Knights Templar?" Maxwell asked.

"Sort of."

Mary was growing more interested in what Dr. Strum had to say. She had questions, but she decided not to press her luck and let him do most of the speaking. However, he did not say anything more.

"Why did you ask us to come here, Dr. Strum?" she asked.

"I am glad you decided to visit and that you are here," he said.

"This is not a damn visit. You beckoned us here. We do not know you. Why are we here?" she repeated.

"Well, a certain group let me know that you two were heading to Rhode Island," Dr. Strum said hesitantly.

"What group?" she asked.

"I really cannot tell you."

"Is that not wrong? You invite us here, and you are basically a stranger. We decided to come to see you, for who knows what, and you cannot tell us how you know us and how you know we came to Rhode Island?" She was upset, and she knew her voice was rising as she spoke.

"It is because of who you are, or who you may be. That is why you are here," Dr. Strum said. He looked down softly, as if a parent had just scolded him.

"What are you saying? Get to the point?" Mary's tone had turned from quizzical to demanding, her posture defensive. Maxwell was surprised at her tenacity.

"Okay, okay, okay … Stop raising your voice," Dr. Strum said, looking down as if he were being scolded again. "What was your mother's first name? Your grandmother's name? And your great-grandmother's?"

Mary paused. "They were all named Mary," she said, as if noticing it for the first time.

"Do you think that was by coincidence?" Dr. Strum asked.

"No," she replied in a more unsure voice.

"No, it is no coincidence," Dr. Strum said, this time looking up and right into her deep blue eyes. "What is your middle name?"

"Beth."

"What is your last name?"

"Mehel."

"Did your parents make you sign an agreement that, if you married, you would not take your partner's last name?" Dr. Strum asked.

Now Mary was growing frightened. "Yes, they did. How do you know that?"

"Did they make you sign an agreement that you would name your first-born daughter after you—Mary Beth Mehel?"

Mary grew silent. She thought the questions about her name and personal life were getting much too strange. *What am I revealing to him?* she thought. *He seems to know much more about me than anyone. Only my parents could have known this.*

"Well, did they?" Dr. Strum asked again.

She felt that he was discussing something that he shouldn't be. He seemed fearful.

"Wait—how do you know this?" Mary asked, her voice becoming softer, timid.

"Have you seen your birth certificate?" Dr. Strum asked more softly as he strolled back and forth behind his desk, as if he was in an interrogation room.

"Not really," she replied.

"I would bet that, on your birth certificate, there is a long Roman numeral following your name. You have no idea how many generations have waited for you."

"*Me?* What does that mean? What are you saying?"

"It means that you are a very, *very* important person in this world."

Dr. Strum looked up at the antique clock on the wall. A handwritten, yellowing flea market price tag was dangling from the bottom. "Oh my, I have to teach an anthropology class in a few minutes." Dr. Strum gathered up some books and grabbed his briefcase off his desk. "I will be in contact with you." He quickly left the office, calling back, "Do not touch anything and show yourself out!" as he scurried down the hallway.

Mary and Maxwell quietly walked back to the car, confused about what had just transpired. Maxwell did not know what to say.

Finally, Mary spoke. "Let's grab a coffee and head back home."

"Okay," Maxwell replied.

Just then, Mary walked past a girl who bumped into her shoulder hard, which caused her to drop the books that she was carrying. Mary bent down to help her pick them up, and as she did, she noticed a tattoo on the girl's neck that read, "*III.*"

"Thank you so much. I am so clumsy," the girl said as she took the books from Mary and straightened. She then continued walking down the path to a bench and sat down between a man and woman. They all watched Mary intensely.

An uncomfortable feeling came over Mary, and she became queasy. She walked quickly to the car, got in, and locked the door.

"Did you see those strange people on the quad looking at me?" she asked Maxwell after settling in.

"No, but that girl seemed to bump into you on purpose—she had plenty of room to pass."

As they drove past the quad again, Mary looked at the bench. They were gone.

Chapter 9

CONNECTIONS

When the phone on the wall rang, Mary walked over to answer it. *Who in bloody hell calls a landline anymore?*

"Hello?"

"Hello, Mary, this is Dr. Strum. Did you guys make it back okay?"

"What? Wait—how in the hell did you get my number?"

"That is not important. I wanted to finish our conversation and tell you more about the origin of your name and who you are. You asked, and now I feel obligated to tell you, even though I may pay a very dear price for giving you the information."

"What are you talking about?"

"Your name," Dr. Strum responded.

"Okay ...?" Mary decided to listen.

"Well, you know that your mother, grandmother, and great-grandmother were all named Mary. What you may, or may not, know is that they had the same middle and last name, also, and it goes back for generations."

"Yes, my mum had the same name as I," Mary said.

"Well, your middle name and last name are especially important. It tells us who you are, or may be."

"I'm sorry, Dr. Strum, but this is a real violation of my privacy, and you are making me very uncomfortable."

Dr. Strum fell silent for a moment. "Mary, shall I continue?"

She did not respond.

"Your last and middle names are coded."

"Coded?"

"Yes, have you ever flipped the letters of your last name and attached them to your middle name?"

"No, you old nut."

"Listen, Mary; this is very serious. I am really putting myself in danger here, even speaking to you. Your middle name is Beth—very common—but when you reverse the letters of your last name, Mehel, and combine it with your middle name, you get *Bethlehem*. That means your full name is Mary Bethlehem, meaning Mary of Bethlehem."

Mary took a pad and pencil from the junk drawer and began frantically spelling her name just as Dr. Stum had described.

MARY BETH MEHEL

LEHEM

MARY BETHLEHEM

Her hand was shaking as she wrote. She did not know what to make of that or of this conversation. She was beginning to think that this guy was really nuts, and that this was some strange coincidence.

"Mary, we believe that you are a descendant of—"

The line went dead.

"Hello?" Mary said. "Hello? Dr. Strum, are you there?"

Mary's heart sank as memories flashed in her head of her mum. She started to get upset. After a few minutes, she regained her composure and dialed Maxwell.

"You must come to my house immediately. Something has happened."

"I'll be right there," Maxwell replied.

After a while, Mary heard a knock at the door. She looked through the peephole then opened the door.

"What happened?" Maxwell asked.

"Dr. Strum called and said my name is really Mary of Bethlehem and that I am a descendant of someone, and then the line dropped." Mary started crying again, and between sobs, she tried to explain what she had been told. "The same thing happened to my mum, and it brought back terrible memories. We were speaking on the phone, and the call just ended with her. My family never saw her again. She just vanished."

"Really? I am so sorry."

"On the call, she said she is an especially important person and that she had to leave for somewhere safe—a safe house. We waited and waited for her return, but she never came back. I was only eleven years old. My dad decided it was too painful to remain in the UK, so we immigrated to the U.S."

Maxwell walked over to Mary and hugged her. "I did not know."

"It's just something that never came up between us, and I do not like speaking about it. What should we do?" Mary asked, crying.

"I don't know. What have we gotten ourselves into?"

The phone rang again. Mary did not want to answer it.

"Please answer that," she muttered.

"Okay." He walked over to pick up the receiver and pressed *Speaker* so that Mary could hear. "Hello?"

"Hello? Who is this?" the voice on the line asked.

"This is Maxwell."

"Oh, fantastic. Maxwell, this is Dr. Strum. I was talking with Mary, and my payphone ran out of money, so I found myself walking through the streets of Downtown Newport, trying to borrow a landline. Can you hear me?"

"Yes," Maxwell replied. "You are on speakerphone."

"I was telling Mary a little bit more about who we think she is—her identity."

"What do you mean? Like her genealogy?"

"No, her origin. Who she *is*. Did she tell you anything?" Dr. Strum asked.

"No."

"Is she there? Can I speak with her?"

Mary shook her head, and Maxwell told him no.

"Okay, I will get right to the point." He paused. "Maxwell, we believe Mary is a direct descendent of Mary, the mother of Jesus."

"*We*? Who's *we*?"

"We is us."

"Say what?" Maxwell asked.

"Dr. Strum, can you be forthright with us?" Mary asked sternly, drawing closer to the speaker.

"Yes, but not on any phone. You will have to come to Newport again," Dr. Strum said.

"Well then, we will arrange it. Goodbye." Mary ended the call.

"What do you think? Should we go back to Newport to meet with the nut?"

"Let me think about it," Maxwell said.

"Okay."

Mary curled up on the couch. She didn't know what to think and had a headache.

She sat up. "I'm hungry. Can we order some food in?"

"Sure," Maxwell replied. "Where are the menus?"

"They are in the junk drawer in the kitchen. Grab the one for Lunch."

Maxwell went into the kitchen and grabbed the menu from the junk drawer. "What is *Lunch*?" he asked.

"It is a great new place. The second location of a quite infamous restaurant that just opened in Southampton. Please just order me the veggie burger and a salad and have them deliver it."

"Okay. What are you thinking, Mary?" Maxwell asked.

"That the conversation we just had with Dr. Strum was just so strange. If it is true, what does it all mean?"

"I agree it was very strange. On the other hand, what if there is some truth to it? Can you think of anything that would validate it?"

Mary thought for a few minutes. "I remember conversations with my mum that could relate."

"Like what?"

"I was so small. I only really remember bits and pieces of conversations, but I remember that she was always speaking about purpose and how special of a person I was."

Mary pulled out a piece of paper and grabbed a pen from the coffee table drawer. She wrote down a summary of the conversation with Dr. Strum as Maxwell walked over to the refrigerator and took out a beer.

He held it up, so Mary could see. "Are these Montauk craft beers good?"

"Yes, very good. Can you bring me one?"

Maxwell grabbed another beer, walked over to where Mary was sitting, and handed it to her.

Mary jumped up and gave him a long hug. "Thank you for being here."

"My pleasure."

Mary was deep in thought as Maxwell tried to lighten the situation.

"How about we watch a movie and try to relax?" he offered.

Maxwell started browsing through the titles and stopped on *The Goonies*. "How about this one?" he asked with a smile.

Mary gave him a sideways look.

He kept going. "How about *Braveheart*? A little history from your homeland, eh? FREEDOM!"

Running out of patience, Mary grabbed the remote from him. It was hard for her to concentrate. All she kept thinking about was her mum, trying to remember their conversations when she had been a child and what Dr. Strum had said. She picked an old *Friends* episode, laid her head on Maxwell's lap, and slowly drifted to sleep.

***

She awoke on the couch, feeling refreshed with the morning sun beaming on her face. She looked around for Maxwell, who was on the floor, sleeping, awkwardly wedged between the coffee table and the couch.

She stepped over him and walked into the kitchen to make coffee.

"What is all that noise?" Maxwell asked, popping his head up from the floor.

"How did you sleep?" she asked as she walked over with a hot cup of coffee.

"Not too good," he said as he sat up. "I feel like a sandwich that someone stepped on. I have an awful kink in my neck."

Mary smiled. He looked so cute. "I love that you slept here."

Maxwell rolled his head to the left then right, trying to work out the kink. "Oh, it was nothing."

"You did not even try to take advantage of me," Mary said, half-jokingly.

"I wouldn't have dreamed of it."

I would have, Mary thought to herself. She was growing more and more attracted to Maxwell.

"I put your food in the refrigerator after you fell asleep."

"Thank you," Mary replied. "What should we do next?"

"How about we take a break from all this and visit the Suffolk History Museum in Riverhead? I've always wanted to go."

"Sounds great. I could use a break from all this, too," Mary replied.

***

When they arrived at the museum, a young fellow at the door asked for a donation. Maxwell placed ten dollars in the basket, and they went in.

The museum was a little gem. It had fascinating displays on past Native Americans, Colonial life, and wars.

"These dioramas are great," Maxwell said as they perused the lowest level. They walked past a display tucked in the corner with Native American pottery. Maxwell stopped in his tracks.

"What is it?" Mary asked.

"Those two tablets. They look like the ones that my uncle showed me in a book he had. He said they were lost. They are supposed to say something about ships coming from Egypt. I am going to call him about this later. Let's go try to ask the curator about them."

Mary and Maxwell went to find the kid sitting at the entrance.

"Excuse me. Is the curator here?" Maxwell asked.

"Yes, she is working on a display in the back room."

"Can we speak with her about an artifact?"

"Sure," the kid said, directing them to a room in the back of the museum.

Upon entering, they saw a woman with brown hair and brown eyes, bent over a display case, arranging artifacts. She stood up and faced them.

"Excuse me," Maxwell said. "May we ask you about an artifact in one of your cases?"

"Sure," she said, bending over the case again to arrange artifacts.

"There are two white tablets on the lower level that appear to have hieroglyphs on them."

The woman stopped what she was doing and faced them again. "Yes, those are plaster casts of a rock found in Orient at Eagle Point," she said.

"Do you know where the originals are?"

"No, sorry, I lost track, but the casts are an accurate copy of the originals."

Maxwell thanked the woman, and then he and Mary proceeded back downstairs. They went to the case, ignored the sign about no photos to the right of the case, and took a few.

"I must show my uncle," he told Mary excitedly.

Photograph of left plaster cast of inscriptions found on boulder, Orient, New York.
Source: Suffolk County Historical Society, Riverhead, New York

Photograph of right plaster cast of inscriptions found on boulder, Orient, New York.
Source: Suffolk County Historical Society, Riverhead, New York

They left the museum after browsing a little more and started driving to Maxwell's apartment through Polish Town. Mary pointed at our Lady of Ostrabama's large church and asked Maxwell to stop.

"I want to go in. Do you mind?"

"Not at all," he replied.

They entered the church, and Mary put her hand on Maxwell's shoulder. "I feel weird," she whispered. "Can you feel that?"

"No. Feel what?"

"I feel ... elated," Mary said. "Like some sort of energy is moving through my body, a charge."

Toward the front of the church, a priest was preparing the altar for an upcoming service. He looked their way then dropped a candleholder, which fell to the floor with a loud *clang*. The priest's head was tilted upward, as if he were looking at something above them. He did not seem to be looking directly at them. He picked up the candleholder and quickly shuffled away. Maxwell decided to ignore it.

Mary sat down in one of the pews, kneeled, and started to pray. Maxwell followed her lead and sat behind her. He marveled at the stained-glass windows and icons placed around the church.

The priest emerged again from behind one of the red curtains with another priest. They were talking excitingly to each other and gesturing toward Maxwell and Mary. Maxwell wondered what all the commotion was about.

After Mary finished praying, she walked over to the prayer candles and lit one. Maxwell knew this was good for her.

As they turned to leave, the church bells started to chime, as if they were being celebrated. Maxwell thought it was coincidental but somewhat strange. Mary paid little attention to them.

Chapter 10

THE RETURN

It was mid-March, a few days before the spring equinox. Maxwell had decided a week earlier to return to Newport with Mary to meet Dr. Strum and learn more about the tower. On the way, Mary spent a lot of time looking out the passenger window. She could not figure out if Dr. Strum was an old creep, nuts, or genuine. What he had said to her had not really sunk in yet. Sure, strange events had occurred in her life, but where was the proof of what he had said? Where was the tangible evidence of her ancestors? What was her purpose? Where was her mum?

What was she supposed to do? Walk into Jerusalem and announce her arrival as Mary of Bethlehem, the one who could see? How ridiculous. She smiled to herself.

Mary then remembered spending time with her mum in their garden in Southwold, eating Mediterranean food, especially Jerusalem olives, her mother's favorite. One day, when she had been about eight years old, she had been lost in her mum's love and radiance as they sat on a garden bench while her mum had brushed her own long, black hair. Her natural beauty, highlighted by the sunlight bouncing off her, had been exuberant. Mary remembered her kind, blue eyes most of all and how she always spoke softly.

"Mary, always embrace your purpose," her mother had said. "It is much greater than you can ever know. Purpose is everything. Without it, we are lost."

"Who is lost?" Mary had asked.

"Humanity. It defines us all—every race, every religion, every culture ... everyone who walked on this Earth." Her mum had then switched the subject to how the hibiscus flowers were brilliant as she cradled one delicately in her hand. The times spent with her had always been filled with love.

After a few hours of driving, Mary and Maxwell neared Newport Bridge. They arrived at Salve Regina University mid-morning, were quickly cleared by security, and proceeded to Dr. Strum's office. He immediately grabbed Mary's elbow and led her out of the building.

"What are you doing?" she exclaimed. "Don't you dare touch me."

"I'm sorry. We cannot speak in my office anymore. It must be outside," he replied. "Some of my colleagues do not, let us say, respect my work and theories as much as they should. They suffer from shortsighted mindfulness."

Mary decided to follow him, only because she knew Maxwell wouldn't be too far behind.

Dr. Strum whisked her to the middle of the quad.

Across the way, she noticed a tall man, in a turban, rapidly approaching from the east with the sun rising behind him.

Dr. Strum let go of Mary and went to meet him a few yards away.

Mary tried to listen in but could only hear what sounded like *Maryam* intertwined with words spoken in an unfamiliar language. She could see that Dr. Strum was nodding his head.

"What do you think this guy is about?" Maxwell asked.

"I have no idea, but he seems harmless enough."

The tall man carried a package under his right arm, and after a few more minutes of conversation, he handed it to Dr. Strum, looked directly at Mary, and smiled. Then he turned around and left.

"We need to go somewhere where we can talk," Dr. Strum said when he returned. "I know that a lot of information was given to you over the past few months, and I can assure you that you are safe."

"Why would you even say that?" Mary asked. "Why would I not be safe?"

Dr. Strum looked a little shocked. His eyes grew wide, and his face flushed. He went to say more but stopped himself.

She got up from the bench and walked away, pacing back and forth for a few minutes before she calmed down. Then she walked back to where Dr. Strum stood.

"Why would I not be safe, Dr. Strum?" Mary asked again.

"Because of who you are." Dr. Strum walked closer to Mary, leaned toward her, and lowered his voice. "You really have to know who you are. You must know who you are." He shook his head as he spoke.

"Who am I?" she whispered.

"Not here. Let's go." Dr. Strum led them to a car on the far end of the quad.

"I am not getting in that car," Mary said. "We really just met you and had a few very strange conversations."

"This is an Uber," Dr. Strum calmly said.

Mary looked at the windshield, saw the stickers and medallions, and then got into the car.

When they were situated, Dr. Strum asked the driver to take them to Touro Park.

Sitting in the back seat, Mary made the sign of a circle near her ear, signaling that Dr. Strum might be nuts. Maxwell shrugged in response.

Touro Park was empty, except for a family taking photos of the tower.

Dr. Strum walked over to an empty bench and sat down. He pulled out a package from his satchel and placed a brown-paper-wrapped box on his lap. "I would like to speak with Mary alone," he told Maxwell.

"Absolutely not." Mary was not having it.

"But, Mary, this is secret information."

"No, he is staying."

Dr. Stum looked at Maxwell, sighed, and then continued, "I would like to show you something." He took two white gloves from his shirt pocket, put them on, and then began unwrapping the package that had been handed to him at the university, revealing a red silk cloth that looked old. He carefully unfolded the cloth to reveal the top of a small wooden box, which also looked old. The patina of the box was dark, and Mary thought she smelled oranges as soon as he unwrapped it.

"It is preserved in orange oil and beeswax," Dr. Strum explained, as if reading her mind. He had tears in his eyes.

On the lid were three crosses incised in a unified pattern, geometrically perfect, and other symbols. A phrase in Latin was also incised into the top.

Dr. Stum took a deep breath then said, "I have been waiting for years to find you and hand this off. Do you recognize the three crosses? The middle one is the Cross of Lorraine."

"No," she replied.

"These are Knights Templar religious symbols, but much more than that. This is a Latin inscription." Dr. Strum angled the box so that Mary could see the inscription. She could not understand what it meant.

Pro illis qui vident

"What does it say?" Maxwell asked.

Dr. Strum took another deep breath and peered into Mary's eyes, leaning in so close that she could feel his breath on her ear. "It says, '*For those who see,*'" he whispered.

"What?" Maxwell exclaimed. "How old is the box, and where did you get it?"

"That's just it," Dr. Strum said. "This box is a holy relic and contained a gift that was given to Mother Mary of Jesus by a king on the day Jesus was born. Mary and Joseph held this box in their hands. Even baby Jesus most likely touched it. The belongings of baby Jesus were most likely stored in it. It has been handed down for generations, over thousands of years, and protected by the Collective."

"The what?" Mary asked, still staring at the box.

"The Collective," Dr. Strum answered.

"Is that another secret order?" Maxwell asked.

"No." Dr. Strum paused for a long time. Then he looked at Mary and said quietly, "It is not one secret order. It is *all of them.*"

Maxwell seemed astonished. Mary found this hard to believe.

"The Collective is comprised of a select group of people, made up of all religions—Christianity, Islam, Buddhism, Hinduism, Judaism, and so many more in all nations, all cultures, for thousands of years. A unified secret order for the sake of humanity."

"But, what about all the wars that have killed millions?"

"Yes, the wars … What were they all fighting for? Their race, their culture, their lands, and existence, and to control what? The one unifying aspect of all of them—the winners and losers, the defense and offense, the aggressors and pacifists—is what?" Dr. Strum didn't wait for an answer. "Humanity. It is humanity.

"The religions teach us forgiveness and to value life. It is not selective; it is not separatist. That is why you are safe, Mary.

You are being watched and protected by every secret, and even non-secret, society, order, and fraternity in the world."

Dr. Strum turned the box so that it was facing Mary. Another smaller set of crosses was carved under a setting sun. "This represents the west," Dr. Strum said. The other side had the same crosses, except the sun was rising. "This side represents the east." He raised the box high into the air to reveal the Star of David on the bottom.

Mary's thoughts switched. "My family! Where is my mum? Do you know where my mum is?"

Someone walking a dog passed them. Dr. Strum waited until the person was far enough away before continuing. "No, Mary," he said, bowing his head. "I am sorry. We do not know where she is, but she is most likely alive and safe."

Mary wanted to believe him, but he sounded unsure.

Dr. Strum handed the box to Mary, and she slowly opened the lid to reveal another inscription in Latin. "What does this say?" she asked.

"It reads, '*Ad omnia est*,' or '*purpose is everything*,'" Dr. Strum said.

Mary thought again about the conversation in the garden with her mum, about her purpose, but then she decided that she'd had enough.

She stood up and began walking down the path without a word, leaving the box and Dr. Strum sitting on the bench.

Maxwell stood up, apologized to Dr. Strum, and then followed her.

In the distance, she could hear church organs. She wanted to find the source. Maxwell seemed to hear them, too, and grabbed Mary's hand. They walked toward a beautiful stone church with a large stone steeple, south of the tower. A sign read, "*Channing Memorial Church*."

They entered, and Mary walked near the front of the sanctuary and sat down. The soft glow of a large, stained-glass window with the words "*Parable of the Sower*" engulfed her and the space in glorious light.

Maxwell felt that Mary needed space, so he looked around the sanctuary to locate the restroom. The sanctuary was stunning, with dark wood and white plasterwork arched ceilings. The stained-glass windows were unsurpassed. He wondered how old the church was as he passed a decree hanging on the wall that read, "*We welcome people from all faiths, traditions, heritages, beliefs, and demographics.*"

He thought about the word that Dr. Strum had said—*humanity*—as he read it.

After a while, Maxwell found Mary, and they decided to return to the hotel.

"Did you see the marvelous stained-glass windows in the church's sanctuary?" Maxwell asked as they walked back to the car.

"See them? I think I felt them."

"Interesting. Well, it's getting late. Can I take you somewhere special for dinner?" Maxwell wanted to destress her after the day's events and talk about what Dr. Strum had said.

"Sure. Where?"

"It is a restaurant called the White Horse Tavern. It is in a Colonial setting."

"Do you think they have a vegetarian dish?"

"I am sure they do. It's the oldest tavern in America. They say it opened in 1673. They had potatoes back then," he said with a smile.

"Let's go then." Mary looked back at the tower one more time before she opened the car door and got in.

Chapter 11

COMPROMISED

The morning Newport weather was moody with fog and rain. Maxwell and Mary packed their belongings then walked down to the lobby to check out. It was raining again, so Maxwell went to fetch the car to pick Mary up at the door. As soon as he pulled up, she ran through the puddles on the ground, emptying them with every wet step. She opened the car door, got in, and began to speak quickly, visibly upset.

"I have to go to England," she began as he started to drive away slowly. "I just got off the phone with my dad."

"Wait—what?"

"I have to go back to England for a while."

"Why?"

"My father said his job has been compromised ... whatever that means."

"What does your father do?" Maxwell asked.

"Something with the CIA."

"*The CIA?* Are you serious?"

"Yes. Why? Is that a big deal?"

"It *is* a big deal," Maxwell said.

"He works in the computer lab. Something to do with cryptocurrency theft."

Maxwell could feel himself flushing and immediately thought about the car that had turned around and the fender bump episode. Could it all be related?

He pulled over to an empty parking space on the side of the road to try to take in what Mary had said. His mind was racing, his stomach churning, and he could feel himself growing more and more anxious.

"What is it?" Mary asked.

Maxwell stared ahead, listening to the rhythmic sound of the windshield wipers as they whisked the water away. "What do we do?"

"I don't know. I must go remote or find a new school and transfer all my classes, or just put the semester on hold. We are leaving at the end of the week."

"The end of the week! Why so soon?"

"I don't know. He would only say that he has been compromised." Mary looked out the rain-blurred passenger window, at the trees softly swaying in the wind. "I am so upset," she finally said.

"I am, too," he said then inwardly chided himself. *Pull yourself together and tell Mary everything will work out.*

"What about our finds?" Mary asked. "What about us? What about ... you?" She turned to look at Maxwell, and he could see tears in her eyes.

"It will work out," he told her, not sure if he believed it. "I have to think on this a while." He noticed a deli at the end of the block. "Would you like me to get you a coffee?"

"Sure."

Maxwell felt that he needed to step away. Thoughts of the past few months' events ran over and over in his head. Had her dad had him followed since he had met her?

He took a deep breath, opened the car door, and sprinted to the end of the block to try to dodge the rain. In a few minutes, he returned with raindrops dotting his shirt and two coffees. Mary was looking down at her phone in disappointment.

"My dad won't give me any further details, and it is so frustrating," she said slowly as she defeatedly placed her phone on the seat next to her.

"Here is your coffee." Maxwell handed her a cup, placed his own in the cupholder, and began to drive.

Perhaps he could follow Mary back to England? Was that even a real possibility? What would it involve? How would she react? All he could think about was how he couldn't lose her. That was out of the question because ...

He realized that he was in love with Mary.

As a strong feeling engulfed him, he looked over at her and gave a reassuring smile. She smiled back through her tears as she raised the hot coffee to her lips.

"I'm a bloody mess," Mary softly said as she put the coffee in the cupholder then pulled out tissues from her purse.

They continued driving from Newport to Stony Brook to catch the afternoon ferry to Orient, New York. The ride was quiet as each of them were lost in their thoughts.

As they neared the Stony Brook campus parking lot, Mary was finishing fixing her makeup.

Maxwell parked then walked to the other side of the car and opened her door. He reached into the glove compartment and pulled out an umbrella for her.

"Oh, I shouldn't," she said. "What about you? You will get wetter."

"I'm fine. Here you go." He handed the umbrella to her. "Let's meet for lunch in the cafeteria around noon, okay?"

"Okay."

Maxwell watched her every step as she walked to the arts and sciences building and disappeared.

***

Maxwell waited and waited at the table for two, expecting Mary to walk through the glass doors at any moment. After a half an hour had passed, he finally decided to order without her, thinking she must be finishing up an assignment.

He got up from his seat and walked over to the serving line to see what the ladies were peddling. Then he wandered over to the refrigerated drinks to see what was available. He opened the cooler door and grabbed an iced tea, paid for it, and then he went back to the table to wait some more. After another fifteen minutes, Maxwell decided to text her.

He waited for a reply.

Nothing.

A little panicked, he tried calling her.

No answer.

He decided to wait another fifteen minutes then go look for her.

He stared at his iced tea, wondering why it was called *iced* when no ice was involved. He finished it then walked toward the arts and sciences building where Mary had class in.

He could not help but think the worse. Had she been kidnapped or hurt?

He quickened his pace down the sidewalk, darted up the building steps, and bolted through the doors. He peered down the hall and, walking quickly, looked into each classroom he passed.

She was nowhere.

Okay, calm down, he told himself. *She could have gotten sick or something.* But, why would she not have texted him about it?

After two hours of looking for her on campus, Maxwell was exhausted. Defeat started to set in. He looked at his phone—his fifteen text messages and ten phone calls had not been answered—and a deep ache developed in his stomach.

His first instinct was to go to the campus security office and file a missing person's report, but he knew it was too early, so he retreated to his car. He decided to sit in the parking lot for another two hours, hoping that, maybe, she would soon knock on the window.

Darkness fell.

Losing hope, he started the car and decided to drive to Mary's house in Southampton. His thoughts were racing, and he did not realize he was doing sixty-five in a thirty-five-mile-per-hour zone until he saw a police car on the side of the road and looked down at his speedometer.

"Shit," he said as he slowed down, passing the police car and checking his mirrors to see if the vehicle had left its ambush spot. It hadn't.

Once he arrived at her home, he knocked on the door.

There was no reply.

She would not just leave me like this, with no text or call.

From what he could see, no lights were on, and the blinds and curtains were shut tightly.

He noticed the security cameras in the eaves and at the front door. He walked to the side yard and peered into the windows, which caught the attention of a neighbor noisily dragging a garbage can down her driveway.

"Can I help you?" the woman asked.

Maxwell backed away from the house. "Maybe. Do you know where the people living here went?"

"No, but earlier today, four black vans and a SUV with tinted windows and serious occupants pulled up and loaded a large number of items from the house," the woman said, now walking back toward her garage. "They were a really strange moving company. They should have brought one big truck." She eyed him carefully. "In any event, I am part of the neighborhood watch, and you look like a nice enough young man … not like the punk riffraff we have around here. So, if you do not want any police trouble, you should leave."

Maxwell took the warning seriously and got back into his car to drive to his apartment. As he passed the woman's house, he could see her dim, shadowy outline looking out the window, watching.

He turned onto County Route 39, his growing concern now turning into a controlled panic. *Black vans? Tinted windows?*

He parked his car then walked up to his apartment, feeling like he had no control of the situation. Not knowing was the worst of all.

Inside, he collapsed on the couch and turned on the TV, but the news was too depressing, so he shut it off and decided to go to bed.

He placed his phone right in front of his face, so close he could feel the heat from the screen. He stayed awake for hours, staring at it, waiting for that familiar *ding* of a text message. He told himself that maybe everything was okay. Since Mary was leaving, perhaps she had to leave sooner for some reason. He closed his eyes, the word *compromised* playing over and over in his mind.

***

He woke early and, with new hope, looked at his phone.
Nothing.

He lay there, watching the sunrise and shadows crawl across the room, but then he had an idea. Maybe he should contact his family. The more people involved, the more it might help him digest the situation.

Maxwell picked up his phone and dialed his uncle. There was no answer, so he left a message. "Uncle, Mary is missing. I was supposed to meet her for lunch, and she did not show up. Her house is dark. Call me." He clicked off then redialed his uncle a few minutes later, figuring he was screening his calls.

"Hello?" Uncle answered.

"Thank God! Uncle, Mary is missing. She was supposed to meet me for lunch, and she never showed up, and she was not at her house. I need some help."

"Maxwell, slow down," Uncle said. "When was this?"

"Yesterday."

"Did you report it?"

"No, I have no standing, and I think it is too soon."

"Okay, you are probably right about that. Did she say anything in the last few days that would have changed her situation?"

"Yes, she said she had to move back to England because her dad was compromised. He works in the cryptocurrency theft unit of the CIA."

"I see," Uncle said. "Well, Maxwell, that is a serious job that can result in serious actions. It seems that Mary had no choice but to follow her dad."

Maxwell calmed down a bit. "Yeah, I guess you're right. She probably had to leave sooner than she thought. What do I do?"

"Nothing. What can you do except wait? Look, do you think she cares about you?"

"Yes, I do. I care for her deeply, also."

"This is out of your control, as hard as it may be," Uncle said. "I think she is okay."

"Thank you so much, Uncle."

"Call me again tomorrow."

Maxwell clicked off the call then glanced at the screen. It was already about noon on Saturday, yet he did not know where to go from here.

He got out of bed and was about to sit down at his computer to look up the cryptocurrency theft unit of the CIA when someone knocked at the door.

Mary!

He ran over to the door and opened it.

It was not Mary. It was a delivery guy for The Roll, a restaurant down the street.

"Delivery," the guy said while holding a bag.

"No, sorry, I did not order anything. You must have the wrong apartment," Maxwell said.

The guy looked confused. He put the bag on the floor to pull out the receipt from his jacket pocket. "No, sir, this is the apartment number—thirteen," he said, reading the order. "It is for one vegetarian salad."

Maxwell's breathing hitched. "What did you say?" Mary had ordered a vegetarian salad when they had first met!

"It is for one vegetarian salad. It's paid for."

"Do you know who ordered it and who paid for it?" Maxwell was growing more excited.

"Man, I just deliver stuff," the guy responded.

"Thank you!" Maxwell reached out, took the bag from his hands, closed the door, and brought it into the kitchen.

It was a sign ... A sign from Mary.

She must be okay, he thought as he opened the bag to see if there was a message inside. There wasn't; only the salad.

The deep ache in Maxwell's stomach returned as he placed the salad in the refrigerator then walked back to his computer.

What does this salad mean? he wondered as he sat down.

He decided not to research the CIA for fear of going down the wrong path. He wanted to focus on finding where Mary could have gone.

He pulled a notebook from his desk drawer and began writing down all Mary had told him about England and what he had learned about her over the past few months.

After a while, he looked at his list.

Southwold

mother is missing

for those who see

holy box

name

This is going nowhere, he thought. He then remembered her friend, Asha, and figured he would contact her through social media. He tried to find her but had no luck. Then he decided to drive out to Mary's house again.

Nothing had changed, and there was no evidence that it was occupied, so he headed to the coffee shop for comfort since it was the place where he had first met Mary.

When he arrived, he walked over to the counter to place his order for a peach tea. He saw that the chair that Mary had frequented was empty. He sat down and sank into it. After a few minutes, the barista brought his peach tea and placed it on the small table to his right.

A young guitar player was setting up in the corner of the room. He pulled his guitar from the case, sat on a stool, and started to play "You and Tequila Make Me Crazy." The notes filled the room in melodic harmony. The guitarist was excellent, and watching him took Maxwell's thoughts off Mary.

When he finished, there was a smattering of applause.

"Good evening, I am Points East," the guitarist said. "Here is an original, 'I'll Get Mine.' I hope you enjoy it."

Maxwell felt himself calming down. He was in his element—drinking peach tea and listening to great music.

I'll have to tell Mary about this later, he thought then caught himself. There would be no later, and that saddened him.

Suddenly, Mary's friend, Asha, walked into the coffee shop and went to the counter, asking for a mobile order.

"Hi, Asha!" he called.

"Oh, hi, Maxwell. Is Mary here, too?"

She did not know that Mary had left. He decided not to tell her.

"No, only me. The music is great, though."

"Sounds great," Asha said as she grabbed a cupholder from the barista. "Well, I have to continue my studies. It's good to see you. Tell Mary hi."

Maxwell watched Asha walk through the door then returned to his chair.

The music started again, but seeing Asha had gotten him thinking about Mary. He found himself constantly checking his phone for any sign of her.

After another half an hour, he decided to head back home. He placed the mug on the counter and began to walk toward the door.

As he passed a sharply dressed young man in all black, wearing sunglasses, seated in a chair next to the door, he heard, "She is gone. Move on."

At first, Maxwell thought the man was speaking to someone else or was on the phone, as he was not looking directly at Maxwell. However, when he looked back at the man through the window while walking to his car, he found the man was looking directly at him.

Chapter 12

ARRIVED

The day began early in the morning, in a whirlwind of instructions and haste as the three SUVs barreled down 495 to JFK Airport. Mary was seated in the back of a black sedan with two prominent, good-looking men in black suits flanking her. They did not say a word as they looked straight ahead, occasionally scanning the surroundings outside the car's dark-tinted windows to check out vehicles pulling up and passing on either side.

"Who are you guys?" she finally asked.

The man on her left pointed to his earpiece and shook his head slowly, as if he was not allowed to answer.

Mary turned around and looked at the car behind them, where her dad was. She didn't know who was in the third car.

They pulled up to the JetBlue terminal, and everyone quickly exited the car.

"My cat, Matt! Where is my cat?" Mary asked as one of the men firmly grabbed her by the elbow to lead her inside the terminal. She noticed that no one was carrying anything except her dad, who was holding a briefcase as they walked.

When she was close enough to her father, she asked, "Dad, where are my cat and our bags?"

"They will follow us. We have our tickets. Let's go to the gate." He picked up the pace.

Near the bathroom, one of the black suits had a young guy pinned to the wall and was trying to take his phone.

"Keep moving," her dad said as they passed them. "People cannot take photos of us, even if we are in their backgrounds."

"We cannot be in the background of someone's random photo?"

"No, we cannot."

"Can I pop in here for a coffee, Dad?" she asked as they passed a Starbucks.

"No, honey, we have to keep moving."

They arrived at the gate just in time and boarded the plane. Four black suits sat all around them. Her dad was not saying much, and the black suits said nothing.

Mary settled between a suit and her dad and tried to calm down. She could feel her heart beating fast. She wanted to withdraw from the situation.

She reached into her purse and pulled out her earbuds, plugged them into her phone, hit her playlist, and closed her eyes to the sound of Coldplay. *This is crazy*, she thought as she sat there, trying to cancel everything out around her. *What does my dad do exactly? How much danger are we in?*

Her dad tapped her on the shoulder. In his hand was a pack of gum. He motioned for her to take one with a half-smile.

She pulled out one of her earbuds. "Isn't this all a little extra? The urgency? The suits?"

"No," he replied. "How is Maxwell?"

"Maxwell? What do you ...? *Ugh*, fine," she said, shocked that he knew about him. She intentionally hadn't mentioned Maxwell because of the way her dad liked to push her boyfriends away from her, and often not even in a subtle way. He would be rude and direct, quizzing them to make them feel uncomfortable, setting ridiculous curfews for her, and insisting he drive them places. It was embarrassing and maddening.

As the plane taxied then eventually took off, everyone seemed to relax a little around her. The suits still were quiet, except to ask the flight attendant for coffees.

Mary thought of Maxwell and how confused he must be and how much she missed him. Her emotions were a cocktail of sadness, excitement, and loss, but she was mostly pissed about how this entire situation had evolved and the little information she had received. She was also pissed that her dad somehow knew about him.

Exhausted from the events, she settled into her seat and drifted off to sleep to the hum of the engines and the sound of her music.

***

"Mary, we're here," her dad said over the sound of Blink 182's "I Miss you."

Mary opened her eyes. She could feel the plane descending.

"Oh, okay," she said, turning off the music. "What time is it?"

"Four a.m."

She groggily sat up, yawned a few times, and pressed the button to prompt the seat to return to the upright position. "Where are we staying?" she asked.

"A hotel. We have a car picking us up."

"Okay." She was still trying to wake up.

The plane landed at Heathrow and taxied to the terminal. The familiar *ding* of the seat-belt-off sign sounded, and her dad rose to retrieve his briefcase from the overhead compartment. With the suits ahead and behind them, they exited the plane.

"Our bags will be delivered, with your cat, to the hotel," her dad said as they walked down the aisle. "When we deplane, we are going to go look for our driver."

"My cat. Thank goodness. I thought you lied and left him, or had someone give him to the neighbor."

"I am not that cruel," he replied.

Once in the terminal, they walked quickly to find their driver. Mary noticed her dad walking toward another black suit holding up a sign that read, *"Bill H."* He had some sort of pin on his lapel. Her dad handed him his briefcase.

That's weird, Mary thought. *Dad's name is Thorsen.*

Her dad glanced behind him and motioned for her to come. She did.

She felt the cold air on her face outside the terminal as they walked to a nearby black SUV and got in.

"Where to, Bill?" the driver asked.

"Yes, where to, *Bill?*" Mary whispered, annoyed that she was still being kept in the dark.

"The Waldorf Hilton."

"Wow, Dad," Mary said. "We are going fancy tonight."

She was angry and excited to be back in England. It brought back a rush of childhood emotions and memories.

Her thoughts switched to her mum as she watched the glow of the streetlights bounce off her lap, one by one, in the morning darkness. She still had hope that her mum was alive and that they would find her one day.

"We are only here two days," her dad, *Thorsen*, informed her.

"Why?"

"Business. We have to keep moving to remain safe."

"*Safe*, Dad?" She looked directly at him, concerned, trying to read deeper into the situation from his expression, but she knew it was useless to try to pry more details from him. She returned to looking out the window.

They arrived, pulling up to the Waldorf Hilton. It was a beautiful area in the middle of the Theatre District with tree-lined streets and stone façade buildings.

The bellhop opened the door, and Mary stepped out. Her dad followed.

A second car pulled up behind them with the suits.

Here comes an entire car of Mr. Personality, she thought.

"They are not staying in our room with us, are they?"

"No, honey," he said as he handed a tip to the driver.

The bellhop opened the building door for them to enter.

She noticed an iconic red telephone booth and smiled as she walked in. She knew she was home, but not for long.

"Checking in?" an attendant asked as they approached the front desk.

"Yes, the reservation is under Bill Hayes," her father said.

"Okay, Mr. Hayes, I see it here. We were expecting you. Suite Room 1307. Take the elevator down the hall to the left." The attendant handed her dad the keys, and then they proceeded to their room.

The elevator ride was extra-awkward with the suits crammed in and the bad elevator music. Mary could not wait to ditch them.

When she opened the door to their room, she gasped at how nice it was. Then two suits barraged past her and proceeded to check the room for who knew what.

Maybe manners and personality, she thought.

The details of the room were impeccable. The room was spotless, and the drapes were open, letting in the morning sun. Vases of fresh flowers were placed about, reminding her of when Maxwell and she had stayed in Newport.

The entire set of *Harry Potter* books was laid out with a signature scarf and hat on the coffee table. Mary pulled out a small book that caught her eye with a jolly pig on the cover, titled *The Christmas Pig*. It was Rowland's first children's book.

She had been a *Harry Potter* fanatic when she was younger, and she wondered if her dad had something to do with this. His gifts always seemed like they were five years behind, as if he yearned for when she had been a little girl. Nevertheless, she was delighted to have the books.

"I am going to take a bath," she told her dad as she walked into the bathroom to check it out. "This bathroom is huge. It almost echoes. There are robes and slippers, too!"

Anxious to feel clean again after the long plane ride, she laid out the robe and slippers, drew the bath, and stepped in. It felt heavenly.

After a few minutes of soaking, she could hear her dad's muffled voice as he talked to someone in the room.

I wonder who that is, she thought as she lay there, staring at the ceiling, thinking of what Dr. Strum had said and about Maxwell and their recent finds. She realized that, without Maxwell by her side, the finds were not so fantastic and the adventures were muted. It was Maxwell who was most important to her now.

A rush of feelings engulfed her, and she began to tear up. She had fallen in love with Maxwell, and now they were lost and out of control. Did all this have something to do with the last few months? She could not help but wonder if there was a connection between the events, the finds, and who Dr. Strum had said she was.

Mary dried off, put on the robe and slippers, and walked into the room, finding her dad on the couch, looking at *The Christmas Pig*. A cart full of food was next to him.

"I ordered food for us," he said. "All your childhood favorites."

The cart was filled with eggs, toast, crumpets, muffins, jam, coffee, and orange juice. She was hungry and eager to eat a good meal.

"Okay, I will eat once dressed. Thank you."

After she got dressed, she walked to the small table near the food cart and began to plate her food, asking, "Who are the suits with us?"

"Sorry, but I can't tell you. They are working for us—personal protection."

"Are they standing outside our door?"

"Yes."

"Why?"

He would not answer, so she decided to change the subject.

"Can we do something today?"

"It depends. What would you like to do?"

"I don't know ... Go to a museum or something. Frankly, I have to divert my mind from a few things."

He was quiet, but then he said, "Okay, we can go somewhere. We'll go to the British Museum. It is secure and nearby."

His silence reminded Mary of how her dad had always seemed strained since her mother had disappeared. Growing up, he would frequently leave her for weeks with the nanny, on business, which had hurt her deeply because he would miss many school events and important things in her life.

Mary thought of all the times when she had sat on stage with her school orchestra, searching the audience for his familiar face, only to be disappointed. The emotions were still unresolved.

Before her mum had disappeared, he had been fun, always joking, taking them on road trips, hikes, and even fishing in Southwold. He had often smiled then. Now she noticed that he rarely smiled and was mostly silent. She felt terrible for him. She felt terrible for *them*.

***

When they arrived at the museum, Mary perked up a little. She had always wanted to go to this museum ever since she had been a girl. It was immense.

She separated from her dad as he spoke on the phone, with two suits in tow as she walked through the exhibits. She gave them names: Bore One and Bore Two. She chuckled to herself every time she saw them.

She grew more excited when she entered a temporary exhibit on the Architecture of Churches and Castles of Early Great Britain with life-size replicas of some buildings. She was impressed with the scale of the exhibit—the hall was enormous.

As she walked through, she could not help but notice the similarity of the construction technique with some of the buildings in America; notably Newport Tower. It was all coming together—the guilds, the architecture, the religious connections, and how civilizations expressed their beliefs in structures built by incomparable craftsmen throughout centuries. She was fascinated with the Knights Templar construction techniques in the exhibit and their similarity with Newport Tower.

The next exhibit caught her interest—a large black and white print of an early etching made by Rosicrucian's that depicted an ark on a mountain and a stone tower structure on wheels, seemingly representing a moveable structure. There were words in Latin throughout.

She read the narrative next to the exhibit and noted that the *"Rosicrucian traced their philosophy and science to the Moors, asserting that it had been kept secret for one hundred and twenty years until the intellectual climate might receive it."*

She looked to see if anyone was around then snapped a photo with her phone.

Her dad texted her that they were going to lunch now and to meet him in the lobby. Bore One and Bore Two already knew the plan and started walking ahead. She was getting hungry and noticed it was approaching midday.

They found a nearby café and sat on the patio near the street. The bores sat at their own table behind them. Mary wondered what the lunch conversation would be like at their table—boring.

Mary repeatedly looked at the photo that she had taken in the museum. Her dad was quiet. She wished Maxwell was there.

Just as she leaned in to take a bite of her salad, she felt a rush of air on her back and a loud crash of bending metal and screeching tires. She turned around and saw that one of the bores was lying on the ground, halfway under a car that had taken out the safety bollards and had crashed into the tables of people behind her. The driver exited the vehicle and started to run down the street.

Mary cowered, terrified, trying to get close to the ground. She watched Bore One take out a gun and fire. She then looked over at her dad, who was crouching down on the other side of the table and saw his face full of fear.

People were lying about, and some were screaming, crying, injured. Tables, chairs, and lunch items were strewn everywhere in the chaos.

The remaining three bores grabbed Mary and ran into the café, asking for a rear door. The manager pointed. Her dad was right behind them.

"Mary? Mary, are you okay? Are you hurt?" her dad repeatedly asked as they ran out of the building and back to the hotel.

"I'm fine, I'm fine. What was that?" she finally said.

No one answered.

The bores surrounded her on three sides as they ran. She looked back at her dad, who had no protection. It then hit her. They were protecting *her*, not him. *She* was their assignment.

Chapter 13

EXPOSED

When they arrived at their room, her dad announced they were leaving immediately and instructed her to pack. The bores guarded the door and called for a car.

Mary was terrified as she threw all her clothes and makeup haphazardly into her suitcase before handing it to a bore, along with her dad's. Then they quickly walked down to the lobby and got into an awaiting black SUV.

"Where to?" the driver asked as they shuffled in, a fourth bore already seated in the car, replacing the one who had been hurt in the crash.

"Train station, please," her dad answered.

"Okay, Mr. Bill," the driver replied.

Mary studied the driver. *Father didn't tell him his name.*

"We must have been exposed here," her dad whispered. "We are now going to France."

Mary just listened. She almost did not want to know the situation.

Her dad made a phone call. All he said was, "Sanctuary Thirteen," and then hung up.

This was happening too fast. What about all those people who had been hurt? Was it because of her?

She started to cry. The bores were emotionless, just watching and scanning.

When they arrived at the train station, her dad said, "Wait in the car," as he went to buy the tickets. He returned shortly and tipped the driver while motioning everyone to follow him.

The train ride to Portsmouth was uneventful, except for a group of nuns staring at Mary from across the aisle. They seemed way too interested in her; their gazes much too long, to the point of being invasive.

The train pulled into the Brittany Ferry terminal, and they proceeded to board. The nuns followed them.

"The crossing is going to take five hours," Thorsen told her as he grabbed his briefcase from the trunk.

"Where are we going?"

"Le Havre, France, to Ligugé, France, then eventually on to Lisbon, Portugal," he said, lowering his voice to a whisper. "We are going to travel to Sanctuary Thirteen first."

"Sanctuary Thirteen?" Mary repeated.

"Yes."

"Dad, come on; stop keeping me in the dark."

He did not reply.

The ferry trip was long and arduous. Mary felt confined to her seat by her dad and the all-seeing bores. She played games on her iPhone on and off most of the way, only pausing to check her texts. She thought about how she yearned to be back with Maxwell in the coffee shop and about how those poor people at the café were hurt, probably because of her.

She looked out the window, saw land ahead in the distance, and decided to get a tea. She got up and walked to the restaurant, with Bore One following. He walked past her and sat his large body down at the table next to her.

"Hey, would you like to join my tea party?"

Bore One gave her a deadpan look and shook his head. "No."

The waiter approached.

"You wouldn't happen to have peach tea and a plate of personality, would you?" she asked the waiter.

At first, the waiter seemed confused. Then he answered, "Yes, I think we do have peach tea, *madame*," he said in broken English. "Take a seat, and I will bring it to you."

She took a seat.

"What kind of music do you like?" she asked the bore. "I like all types of music," she continued when he did not respond. "But my absolute favorite is Hans Zimmer ... I think he is connected to the cosmos. You know, a doll would be better than you at my tea party—they are much prettier."

He did not answer, though she did see a half-smile form on his face.

"Ah, you do have a sense of humor."

She grew bored of the game and decided to check her phone messages. Most were from Maxwell, her friends, and professors asking about her wellbeing. She saw one from Asha saying that she ran into Maxwell in the coffee shop and that he looked and sounded a little sad. "*Are you guys okay?*" she had texted.

If she only knew, Mary thought to herself. The lack of communication was becoming a real struggle.

She was under strict instructions from her dad that she not communicate with anyone. He kept reiterating that, "All our lives may depend on it." After what had happened at the café, Mary believed it and took the situation they were in even more seriously.

The waiter arrived, placing a steaming cup of peach tea down in front of her. The sweet smell brought back good memories.

Mary finished her tea, watching the people around her, when the sound of the ferry horn startled her as it announced their arrival at the port. Mary put her phone away and hurried back to her dad, who was preparing to disembark.

"Did you find your tea?" he asked.

"Yes."

Once on land, they quickly walked through the terminal with the bores surrounding them. One was carrying Matt in a cat carrier; she could see him bobbing up and down through the vent holes. He smelled terrible.

She walked up beside him. "Matt, where have you been? I missed you." She stuck her finger through one of the holes to give him a short pet.

At the curb, they waited as two black SUVs pulled up in front of them. They shuffled into them as the driver placed their luggage in the back. Her dad sat next to her in the back seat with a bore.

She turned around and looked back at Matt. "Did you have a good trip? Were these big men mean to you? I think we will rename you Pew," she said, waving her hand in front of her face.

Looking past Matt, she was surprised to see four nuns getting in the SUV behind them.

"Sanctuary Thirteen," her dad said to the driver.

"Words?" the driver asked.

Her dad took out a piece of paper and a pen from his top pocket and wrote down, "*Monk*," "*Wear*," "*Mouth*," "*Jarrow*," and "*Northumbria*." Then he handed the paper to the driver.

"Hi, Bill, good to see you again," the driver said as he checked his mirrors before pulling away.

Mary rolled her eyes. "Dad, the four nuns?"

"Yes, they are with us."

She decided to test him. "With the Collective?"

Her dad quickly glanced at her but said nothing for a while. He seemed deep in thought, and annoyed. "Yes," he reluctantly mumbled, as if Mary knew something that she should not. "They are Saviors, a different kind of protectors."

"For me?"

"Yes."

"None of this is for you, Dad? It is all for me?"

"Yes. Sorry I could not be forthright with you," he said apologetically. "You are an extraordinary person, like no other on this Earth."

"So I've heard," she said, thinking about Dr. Strum.

"From whom?" her dad asked, but then said, "Never mind. It does not matter now. We'll be in Paris soon."

"Dad, those people in the café ..."

"I know. It was tragic. I feel bad. Everyone is going to be okay, according to my sources. The bollards did their job."

Feeling a little safer, Mary leaned her head against the glass window and watched the farms and cottages pass. Thoughts of her mum returned, and she wanted to press her dad some more on what had happened to her, but she knew it was not a good time.

"Dad, who am I?" Mary asked softly.

"You are ..." He stopped himself. "Can I tell you later?" He motioned to the people around them with his head.

"Please answer me."

She noticed the driver staring at her in the rearview mirror.

"Eyes front, driver, please," she said, annoyed.

"Driver, can you play some music?" her dad asked.

The driver complied, turning on a local French radio station.

"You are Mary, my daughter, and a very special person in this world, but I cannot tell you how until later."

"So, why all the protection?"

"It is because of who you are—your genetic lineage."

It was all making better sense now—the incidents where Maxwell thought people were staring, Dr. Strum and his rant, and the speed in which they had left the United States.

"Well, if you are going to tell me that I am some sort of descendent from a holy icon and I have superpowers, then I will need much more convincing. I feel nothing, except loss now."

Thorsen jerked his head back in surprise, wondering what she had heard. "I am also filled with loss. I miss your mum so much."

Mary looked at him. It was the first time that he had ever mentioned one of his feelings to her.

She laid her head on his shoulder and grabbed his hand as the SUV sped along to their next destination.

Chapter 14

CRASH

A small sign read, "*Graville Abbey*," and the buildings looked old in the low sun as they pulled into a courtyard.

"Is this Thirteen?" Mary asked.

"No, but we are going to stop here for the men and women to check-in, eat, and then we will be on our way. You should eat here, too, because we will not be able to stop once we are on the highway. We will have to keep moving."

As they exited the vehicle and walked to a large wooden door, she wondered how the driver had known to drive them to this place. No directions had been given.

Her dad knocked on the door, and a small window opened.

"*Nam qui vident*," her father said, and the person behind the window closed it without a word.

They waited a few minutes, and then the door was opened with an iron *clang* and a long, slow *creak*. Before them stood a monk.

He reached out and, in perfect English, said, "Bill, welcome. Come in."

Not one person on this trip had addressed her, or even asked her name.

As they walked into the entryway, the monk asked if they were hungry and motioned to two other monks standing in a doorway. They entered a large, magnificent cathedral hall with long wooden tables and chairs.

As they took seats at one of the tables, the two monks emerged with a pitcher of water, bread, cheeses, and fruit on a long wooden board. They placed the food down in front of Mary.

"*Mademoiselle*, a charcuterie board for you, complete with Jerusalem olives and no meat," the monk proudly stated, not making eye contact. He seemed aware of her significance. Mary had noticed that his hand had shook as he placed down the board. She looked up quickly, surprised when he recoiled.

"They know I am a vegetarian?" she whispered to her dad, who was seated across the table. "How? And the olives?"

He did not answer as he took a bite of cheese and grabbed an olive from a small wooden bowl.

Mary was too hungry to press him and decided to have a piece of each item.

The monk who had greeted them and who had excused himself after they had seated themselves returned with an small, old wooden box that smelled of oranges. Mary immediately recognized it. It was much like the one Dr. Strum had tried to give her in Touro Park. How could there be another here?

"*Mademoiselle*, for you," the monk said as he stretched out his arm to hand it to her.

Mary hesitated, looking over at her dad, who was chewing. He motioned with his head for her to take it.

As she placed it on the table, another monk appeared at the far end of the hall, excitedly speaking in Latin and making wild gestures with his hands.

"Mary, we have to go," her dad said suddenly. He stood up, stuffed more bread and cheese into a cloth napkin, and popped an olive into his mouth.

"Okay," she said, slowly grabbing the box and placing it in her purse.

Behind the monk, the bores and nuns were approaching in quickstep. They met them and continued walking down the long hall to the waiting SUVs. Mary could see glimpses of a river as they sped out of the parking area and through the side streets.

Once they were on the highway, everyone seemed to relax a little. The scenery was lovely, accented by rolling hills and wide-open views illuminated by the setting sun. It seemed like they were moving too fast as they passed car after car. Mary looked back, seeing the second car was right behind them.

She was watching the scenery out the side window when she heard the bore seated in the passenger seat shout, "Turn!"

Up ahead, coming over a hill, were two approaching headlights in their lane.

Mary screamed as her dad grabbed her and shoved her to the floor.

"Turn!" the bore yelled again, louder than before.

The car was jerked then careened off the road through a barbed-wire fence, bouncing into a field of cattle, which scattered in all directions.

There was a loud crash of bending metal, and after the car stopped, Mary looked out the rear window. The second SUV had collided with the truck head-on. Smoke was pouring from both vehicles, and flames were building. Debris was everywhere, and there were silhouettes of people lying in the roadway, outlined by the dimming sunlight.

"Is everyone okay?" her dad asked.

"Yes, but I bumped my head on this guy's shoulder," Mary said, rubbing it. "I'm okay."

The bores and her dad quickly exited the car and ran to the scene.

She had to get out, too. This was way too much for her to handle, and she needed air before she passed out.

Stepping out, she heard a cow in distress to her right. She looked over and saw a calf lying on the ground, kicking the air with three legs, and trying to get up, its fourth leg looked broken and angled in the wrong direction. The car had probably hit it, and it was obviously in pain.

Mary walked over to the calf and placed her hand on its chest. She could feel its rapid heartbeat and short, panicked breaths. One black eye looked up, wide with terror.

"*Shh* ... It's all right," she said as she stroked its chest then touched the thigh and leg that was not moving. "*Shh* ... little one. It's okay."

She felt the cow's heartbeat begin to slow down and its breathing becoming deeper and more rhythmic. It stopped kicking, and the distressed cries ceased as it lay there, continuing to stare at her with its one black eye.

"There is nothing we can do, Mary. Get back in the car!" her dad shouted as he jogged back from the accident with three bores in tow.

"Nothing?" Mary asked.

"No, they served their purpose, as they should."

Mary suddenly realized that her dad wasn't talking about the cattle. He was speaking of the nuns.

"Just too many were taken at once, but there may be one less because of them."

"How cold, Dad. One less what?"

Her question was met with the familiar silence that her dad had developed during this trip.

As Mary thought about the nuns, the driver, and the calf, a wave of deep sadness moved through her, followed by a rush of overwhelming peace. She said a small prayer for them.

"Driver, get us out of here," her dad commanded.

The driver put the SUV into reverse and backed up to where they had left the road.

Mary looked straight ahead and noticed that the calf was now standing up and taking a few steps as the headlights illuminated the field.

The feeling of peace remained.

Chapter 15

HOPE

Maxwell pulled into his uncle's driveway then approached the door. He could hear Amerock eagerly barking and scratching inside as he knocked.

His uncle opened the door and gestured for him to come in, and Amerock, tongue hanging out and tail wagging, jumped on Maxwell as if he was the one that Maxwell had come to see. Maxwell knelt down and petted him for a few seconds.

"I remember when all this dog did was nip at me," he said, rising.

"Yes, he has gotten better," his uncle said as they walked to the table and sat down.

Maxwell noticed his uncle was still limping. "Hip still bothering you?" he asked.

"Yes, when the fronts come through." Uncle seemed more serious than usual. He took out his pipe and lit it. "Well, any news on her?"

Maxwell looked down. "No, I am beside myself. I do not know what to do next."

"Hmm ..." his uncle hummed as acrid smoke began to fill the space. "I think you need to go over there and look for her. Everyone leaves a trail."

"I do not know where to begin."

"Well, think about it ... Remember you were interested in Newport Tower? I found more during my research on it," his uncle said, abruptly changing the subject.

"Yes."

Uncle got up and limped over to the radio. He turned up the volume.

Here we go again, Maxwell thought.

Uncle sat back down and pulled out a large map of the eastern shoreline of the United States. A straight, dark line was drawn from Newport Tower, north, to the money pit on Oak Island.

"What does this say?" Uncle pointed to the endpoint.

"*Oak Island*," Maxwell read aloud.

"Yes, Oak Island. I have a theory that Newport Tower is connected in some way to Oak Island."

"How? A marker or a map?"

"That is for you to discover, nephew. I just develop the theories."

Maxwell thought about it. "Like the same group of people?"

"Could be," his uncle said as he exhaled, adding more smoke to the space. "Take the map, study it, and let me know what you find."

"I am only interested in finding one thing now, Uncle."

"I know." Uncle leaned up and placed his hand on Maxwell's shoulder. "I have invited someone over who I would like you to meet that may be able to help. She has contacts in Europe."

Over the next half hour, Uncle recanted various tales of his discoveries, making a point again to say that he knew the Vikings had been here, in North America, way before the recent finds said they had been. He reminded Maxwell of the ship petroglyph.

"I found something you are really going to like." Maxwell reached into his pocket and pulled out an envelope of the photos that he had taken of the tablets at the Suffolk County Historical Society. He was just about to show them to his uncle when there was a knock at the door.

"Maxwell, please answer that."

Maxwell rose and left to open the door. Standing before him was a striking older woman with a dark complexion that framed her light green eyes. Her long, black hair flowed out of the hood of a royal blue cloak, closed with a silver cross clasp across her breasts. On her right breast was a silver pin that looked like the letter "*C*" with a cross within it. Maxwell was stunned. She looked like someone you would expect to see at a Medieval reenactment event, certainly not in Southold.

"May I come in?" she asked in an English accent.

"Oh, yes." Maxwell stepped aside to let her pass.

She walked in and stood next to his uncle, fanning the air to rid it of smoke.

"Gaspar, smoking will kill you," she said.

"I know," Uncle replied.

Gaspar? Who the hell is that? Maxwell thought.

"Gaspar is my name known to this group," he said, as if reading Maxwell's mind. "One of the Three Wise Men from the East."

"What?"

"Not important," his uncle said. "Maxwell, this is Mattea. She may be able to help us with locating Mary."

"How?"

"Go with her to Europe. I promise she will keep you safe, and you will learn more ancient history than any academic can teach you."

Maxwell was confused and skeptical, but he trusted his uncle more than most in his family. He seemed to know so much.

"Will you go, Maxwell?" his uncle asked.

"Yes, I guess so."

"There is no room for guessing here," his uncle said sternly, raising his voice. "It's either yes or no."

Maxwell paused. This seemed so sudden and too complicated. He had school and an internship, but he knew in his heart that he must go and try to find Mary.

"Yes, I will go. I need to go home and pack, grab my passport, tell my job, and let my professors know I am switching to remote learning for the remainder of the semester."

"Great, then," his uncle said, slamming his hand down on the table and causing Amerock to startle. "Go then. I need to speak to Mattea. I will give her directions to your apartment."

He then turned to Mattea. "Guard him with your life. You know how special he is."

"I will."

***

Mattea arrived at Maxwell's apartment and helped him load his bag.

"Always watching," she whispered to herself when she noticed they were being watched by a man in a parked car.

Maxwell came down the stairs and entered the waiting car. "Can I ask where you are from?"

"I am from the holy land. I was orphaned as a little girl in India and ended up in a convent in England. Before I moved there, my family lived in poverty along the railroad in India. They were killed by a passing train trying to save my little brother. He died, too. A nun saw me on the street, wandering aimlessly, and brought me to the holy land."

"My God, I am sorry that happened to you.

Mattea lowered her head. "Me, too."

Chapter 16

CONFESS

The SUV continued speeding toward Sanctuary Thirteen. Everyone was still on high alert.

Mary began planning on how to approach her dad with all her questions. There were many, starting with her mum's disappearance and the incidents with Maxwell thinking he was being followed. Then there was the mysterious, staring men at the coffee shop and Parrish Art Museum.

She had seen a change in her dad. He had grown more silent in response to her inquiries. The events over the past few days were serious. However, she was not a child and deserved to know just what the situation was; how dangerous it was.

"Dad, you need to tell me more. I deserve to know what this is all about."

He looked over at her. "You're right. I have been protecting you all your life; maybe now is the time for you to know." He paused. "I am really not supposed to tell you, but ..." He then leaned closer to her ear and faintly whispered, "Mary, you are a holy descendant of the Virgin Mary."

"How do you know that? Have you been speaking to crazy Dr. Strum?"

"Who is he?" her dad replied. "And no." Then he whispered again, "The lineage of Mary has been recorded for thousands of years by monks across the world in an organization known as the Collective. I will tell you more later when we arrive at Sanctuary Thirteen."

"Oh my God ... Dad, you're impossible" She was growing tired of his secrecy.

The remaining drive was calm and quiet.

***

They arrived at Sanctuary Thirteen in the early morning hours. The adrenaline from the crash had worn off, and Mary had fallen asleep on the ride until the stopping of the SUV awakened her.

"We are here," her dad announced.

"Where?"

"Ligugé Abbey," her dad said as he exited the car. "Thirteen."

From what she could see in the dark, it was a large, sprawling building complex.

"Hurry," her dad said as three monks rapidly approached the vehicle. "They will show us to our rooms."

They walked upstairs to a second-floor hallway with stone floors, each loud step reverberating into the distance, announcing their presence.

"*Mademoiselle*, this is your room," a monk said as he opened the door. The room was small and nondescript, simply decorated with a bed, nightstand, desk, and chair. A plain wooden cross hung on the wall above the bed to the left of a small window.

"Mr. Bill, your room is right next door. Follow me, please."

Mary could not believe that even they knew her dad as *Bill*.

She shut the door and collapsed on the bed, trying to forget her experienced terrors. She thought she heard her dad talking to a female through the wall as she lay there. All she could make out was her dad saying, "... not a good idea. She cannot handle it."

She was wide awake, staring at the ceiling for some time, when she got up, paced around the room, sat at the desk, checked the walls for peepholes, looked out the window, lay back down, and began to devise a plan on how to leave the abbey. She knew she needed to leave this situation. People around her were getting hurt and dying, and she could not handle it anymore.

She rose out of bed a second time, still dressed, and grabbed her shoes, placing them under her arm. She did not want to put them on for fear of someone hearing her footsteps in the hallway.

Slowly opening the door to her room, she stepped out into the hall. Subdued candlelight from small fixtures, placed at even intervals, barely illuminated the highly polished floor. She could see a large wooden door at one end and decided to head toward it.

Just as she reached for the doorknob, a massive figure stepped out from an enclosure, holding a lantern. She stepped back, startled.

"Hello," the figure said, his baritone voice bellowing down the hall, his body looming over hers. He held up a lantern.

"Oh, hello," Mary said. "I did not see you there."

"Where may you be going this early in the morning? Breakfast is not served for another two hours."

Mary did not have a good answer and remained silent.

The man stretched out his oversized hand toward her. "Hi, I am Augusto."

"I am Mary."

"I know." He leaned in closer, lowering his voice. "Nice to meet you. Are you hungry? Were you looking for food?"

"Yes," Mary lied. She *was* a little hungry and thought that if she saw more of the abbey, she could make a plan on how to leave.

"I am not supposed to leave this post, but let's go see what we have in the kitchen cupboards." Augusto started walking his massive body down the hallway, motioning for Mary to follow him. "I am very excited you are here," he said. "You are more beautiful than I imagined."

At the other end of the hallway, Augusto opened another wooden door, and they stepped into a large kitchen that was dark and stone cold. He turned on the lights and apologized for the temperature. "It warms up quickly when the ovens are full and baking." He opened a large wooden cupboard and took a loaf of bread from the shelf. "Is this good?"

"Yes, thank you."

He placed the bread on a wooden plate then pulled out a jar of strawberry jam from a nearby icebox. "Here you go." He handed the items to Mary.

Mary took the bread and jam from him as he reached into another drawer and handed her a dull knife.

"I must get back to my post," he said.

"Sure."

"Follow me." Augusto began the walk back to his post in the enclosure, but he stopped at the door of her room. "If you need anything, find me."

"I will. And thank you."

This was the first time Mary had been comfortable with a person, besides her dad, on this trip. She could tell that Augusto was everything good in a man. He looked directly at her when he spoke, which was a first from everyone whom she had encountered, he did not seem intimidated by her, and there was a poignant sincerity about him.

As she sat there, eating her bread and jam, she wondered who her dad had been speaking with. She also wondered how

Maxwell was doing and where Matt was. Everything she cared about seemed to have been removed from her life, one by one, starting with her mum. She was growing weary of loss and these circumstances, and she suddenly thought that Augusto might be able to help her.

She finished her bread as the early morning light began to fill the room through the small window. She peered out and could see dew accenting the trees.

Suddenly, there was a slight knock at the door. She opened it a crack to see who it was and found a small monk with a steaming cup of coffee.

"Good morning, *mademoiselle*," he said in a high-pitched voice as he walked into the room and set the coffee down on the nightstand next to Mary's empty plate. "Oh, I see you had an early-morning snack. I will take the plate to the kitchen and come back to take you and Mr. Bill to the dining hall for breakfast in a few minutes. The abbot is very excited that you are here and wants to meet you."

"Can I ask you if there are any other women here, besides me?"

"No, *mademoiselle*. Not allowed. Just you."

The small monk hurried off down the hallway in the direction of the kitchen. He returned a few minutes later as her dad stepped out into the hallway, stretching.

"Please, follow me, *mademoiselle* and Mr. Bill."

He led them into the dining hall that was bustling with monks pulling out long wooden benches to sit down at a long wooden table. The small monk motioned for them to be seated near the head.

Soon, everyone stood up as a man entered the room and was announced—Abbot San Frisco De Cordana.

The abbot motioned with his hand for all to sit, and everyone followed. He then led them in prayer. On the word *Amen*, the room erupted with people eagerly grabbing at the food items centered on the table.

Mary had a feeling that this breakfast was much more special than usual. She looked around for Augusto, but he did not seem to be in the dining hall. With his size, he would be hard to miss.

"I am so excited you are here," the abbot said to Thorsen as he took a bite of his toast. "We have been waiting and preparing for many years—of course, in secrecy—to meet and protect her. My monks are trained in many skills that could accomplish that, if needed. Mr. Bill, you know we—"

"Yes, I have seen the films," her father interrupted. "I know monks are trained and talented."

As they continued to talk, Mary began to think that her dad had been here before. The conversation was too comfortable.

"Sir, can I ask where the monk, Augusto, is?" Mary asked the abbot.

Abbot San Frisco De Cordana set down his coffee and grabbed a piece of bread. "Who?"

"A man named Augusto," she said. "He stands about seven feet tall ... He's hard to miss."

"I am sorry, Mary. We have no monk by that name here."

Mary was puzzled. He had been there only a few hours earlier, helping her. She decided to ask another monk later in the day, if she had a chance.

The rest of the breakfast conversation focused on the history of the abbey and the gardens. Mary noticed that many of the monks were looking in her direction, as if she was on view.

"Tomorrow, we will have lunch in the garden with the abbess Isabella Maria Barachie from the local convent. Feel free to explore the monastery, except for the lower cellar. The library is magnificent," the abbot said. "Now, if you will excuse me, I have unexpected business to tend to." He rose from his chair. "It has been nice meeting you all. May God bless and keep you."

***

Abbot San Frisco De Cordana exited the dining hall and scurried down three flights of stairs to the lower cellar, where, among the old wine bottles and cured meats and cheeses hanging from the rafters, there was a large bed jammed into the corner. In it, Augusto was facing the wall, sleeping. The abbot shook him.

There was no response.

He then picked up a piece of a stave from a broken barrel and whacked Augusto on the ass.

"*Ow*," Augusto said.

"Augusto, you fool! Did you interact with Mary? Have you lost your mind? You are a silent sentry ... not to be seen or heard by anyone. A sentry in the night!"

Augusto rolled over. "Do you know how big I am? I am not supposed to be seen? Ever?"

The abbot whacked him again.

Augusto stood up, his head almost touching the ceiling, and looked down at the abbot, who stepped back as Augusto grabbed the wooden stave from his hand and crushed it. "Do not hit me again—ever, Abbot," Augusto said.

"I am sorry, but you are a silent sentry because you have no talents. You cannot sing, let alone remember the hymns. You cannot chant well, and you are a slow speaker. That is why we made you a silent sentry. It's a critical position."

"A very lonely position," Augusto added.

"Nevertheless, do not interact with Mary, or any of the guests, or I will have you before the board." The abbot turned to leave the room.

"God accepts my faults. Why can't you ... Papa?" Augusto asked.

Abbot San Frisco De Cordana spun around, his cheeks burning. "Do not ever call me that again!" He turned then continued walking.

"God loves all people unconditionally. It's man's religious beliefs and stigmas that have divided us, you *bigot*."

The abbot paused at the word *bigot* before slamming the cellar door behind him.

Augusto had never said anything like that before to anyone. The abbot wasn't even sure Augusto knew what a bigot was. He had always been fearful—fearful of the unknown, the holy repercussions, the labels.

Augusto looked around his room. The foul stench of meat and cheese permeated over everything in the dampness. He knew he had to leave this place. He was tired of living in the cellar. He knew his papa would never accept him and would constantly dwell on his faults, whether they were real or fabricated.

He sat back down on the bed and took a deep breath. He felt different—not so stoic and clearer in mind ever since he had encountered Mary earlier that morning. And it worried him.

Chapter 17

EXIT

Mary was awakened by the sound of voices and footsteps rushing by in the hall. It was still dark outside. She had a feeling that all was not well in the monastery.

She pulled on her shoes and crept to the door. Opening it slightly, she saw several monks gathered near the large, wooden door and the enclosure where she had met Augusto. Realizing this was her chance to see him again and validate that he was real, she decided to walk down there.

"What is going on here?" she asked as she approached the circle of men.

No one answered, but she was used to that.

She turned and saw Augusto seated on a bench. He looked up, and she saw tears had left trails down his cheeks.

"I ask again … What is going on here?" She looked directly at an older monk standing closest to Augusto. His posture was defensive, with one foot forward and one back.

"*Mademoiselle*, this is an incident of the abbey," he said, never taking his eyes off Augusto. "I am sorry, but you should return to your room, please."

"Incident? Augusto, are you all right?"

"Yes, I did something I was not supposed to do. I will be okay."

With his reassurance, she decided to return to her room, although she was determined to find him later, even if she had to search the entire abbey.

She lay back down on her bed but could not go back to sleep. The feeling of leaving the abbey was much more intense after seeing Augusto upset.

I will ask Augusto to come with me, she thought. *He knows the area, and I do not. Besides, he is a menacing man with his size, and I do not think anyone would dare approach us.*

She yearned to return to the States and Maxwell. Her heart ached as she lay there, awake.

***

The hall grew quiet. She decided to put her plan into action. Already dressed from the "Augusto incident," she took off her shoes and placed them under her arm as she crept out the door once more.

There was no one else in the hall as she walked toward the enclosure, hoping to encounter Augusto. He was there, looking more solemn now. He did not confront her as she approached.

"Augusto, what happened?"

He looked up at her. "Frankly, Mary, I am unsure. After our encounter yesterday morning, I started feeling different. A sense of deep peace and clear mind washed over me. I started to remember things I buried years ago—good and bad, pain and forgiveness. I remembered how one of the brothers had mistreated me as we grew up, always saying things that would hurt me deeply. When we would practice martial arts, he would never pull his punches, saying a big goon like me could take it and laughed as my face bled. The abbot would often witness this and did nothing, which I never understood.

"Last night, I was making my rounds and noticed the brother was on wash duty ... That is when you must wash the floors in the abbey at night. I walked by in peace, but he took the opportunity to criticize me again. I turned to him and laid him out flat with one great punch, and let me tell you, I did not pull it. Of course, he reported me to the elders, so I must report to the council in the morning."

He waited for a reaction from Mary.

"Good. You did the right thing by standing up for yourself," she said. "I am thinking of leaving the abbey."

"What for? A walk?"

"No, I will not return. I am putting everyone here in danger."

Augusto sat up straight. "I cannot let you leave alone. You are a very special person, and I must protect you at all costs. After all, I am the silent sentry."

"The what?"

"Never mind. I do not think it is even a thing. I will leave with you," he said, standing as he outstretched his hand.

Mary grabbed it. "Brilliant," she said. "Go grab your things, and I will try to grab mine."

Mary returned to her room and realized she had nothing to grab except a few clothes laid out from her luggage. She gasped when she noticed someone had placed a royal blue cloak with a gold cross clasp on top of the desk chair.

She took out a piece of paper and pen from the side table and wrote down a quick note to her dad.

> *Dad,*
>
> *Taking a break from all this. I am leaving for a bit.*
>
> *I will contact you soon.*
>
> *Love,*
>
> *Mary*

She placed the pen down, finished stuffing the clothes in a knapsack, put on the cloak for warmth, and left the room. She walked down the hall to wait in the enclosure for Augusto.

After a few minutes, Augusto returned with a large burlap sack, labeled "*Café*," strung over his shoulder. She smiled at him.

"We have to avoid the bores," she explained. "Is there a back door that would place us closer to the river?"

"Yes, follow me."

As they began to quickly walk down the hall, Augusto asked, "Who are the bores?"

"They are my security detail ... They have the character of cold stone."

They reached another wooden door.

"Here, this will lead to the rear of the building." Augusto opened the door, and they stepped into the open air and darkness.

She could see a dull glow on the horizon—the rising sun.

As they walked out of the courtyard, she noticed cameras in the eaves. "The cameras," she said, a little panicked.

"Oh, do not worry about them. Brother Santiago monitors them. He is pushing ninety-five years old and usually naps in front of the monitors," he assured her then said, "Let's head for the train station to the north."

"Great," Mary said, feeling free.

"Do you have any money?" Augusto asked.

"Yes, I have some."

They jogged down the narrow streets and eventually arrived at the train station. She noticed the village was waking up, and more and more vehicles were on the roadways. She thought she saw a bore pass the station window on a moped, looking quite ridiculous in a full suit as he stopped in front. Worried, she pulled Augusto into the ladies' room and into a stall to hide until the train started boarding.

She heard a woman come in after them. Immediately after, she heard the door open again and the heavy footsteps as the bore tried to enter. He took a few steps in, and the woman noticed him and started yelling.

"Get out of here, you creep! Creep! Security! Security!"

The bore quickly shut the door and left the station. He could not risk blowing his cover.

Chapter 18

ABBESS

The abbess Isabella Maria Barachie stepped out of the car and into the midafternoon sunlight, illuminating the golden cross clasp securing her royal blue cloak. She was young and beautiful, not the youth one would expect from such a powerful woman. With composure and grace, she straightened and walked toward Abbot San Frisco De Cordana, who was standing near the entrance, nervous and sweating. He wiped his brow with a cloth as she approached.

"Abbess, I have news."

"Oh?" she replied as she walked past him and through the large wooden doorway. He followed.

"Uh ... The special lunch guest left the abbey early this morning." The abbot's voice cracked as he spoke.

Isabella stopped walking and turned to face the abbot. "What, San Frisco? She left ...? For what? Why?"

The monks standing around him had their heads hung low.

"We do not know, but we think she is with Brother Augusto, one of our silent sentries. Her own security detail is out looking for her." He hoped that would instill confidence in her that Mary was safe.

"What is a silent sentry?" Isabella asked. "I have never heard of such a ridiculous thing."

"Never mind," Abbot De Cordana said, embarrassed, knowing it was a title that he had conjured up for his son.

Isabella remained composed and said nothing more, her disappointment evident as she headed back through the doorway to her waiting car.

San Frisco was mortified. He knew the outcome of Mary leaving would not be good for him.

He clapped the monks standing around him into action. "I want all of you to scour this village for Mary. You have all seen her during breakfast, so you know what to look for. Brother Augusto may be with her, and he cannot be missed."

"Yes, Abbot," they all said in unison as they scattered in all directions.

***

Isabella smiled to herself as the car pulled away, knowing that the abbot's misfortune presented a new opportunity for the convent.

The vehicle soon pulled through the convent gates, passing the familiar small brass sign that read, *Collegium Sororis Salomonis.*

Stepping out of the vehicle, she asked a ranking sister to immediately convene everyone in the main chapel.

"Everyone, Mother Superior?" the sister asked.

"Yes," she responded, and the sister scuttled off.

By the time Isabella reached the chapel, it was crowded. She motioned for all the nuns to sit. Because the meeting was unusual, they seemed excited to be diverted from the day's chores and obligations.

"Sisters, we have a unique opportunity to find an extraordinary person, one who we have been waiting decades, even centuries, for," Isabella began. "Please head into the village and look for a woman named Mary. She is most likely wearing one of our cloaks that I confidentially sent to her earlier. If you find her, please convince her to come to the convent for her own safety. If she refuses, remain with her always." She paused. "Another thing ... She may be with Brother Augusto from the monastery. If you remember from our socials, he is a very large man. We will break into groups for the search."

The sisters exited the building, giggling and chattering excitedly, as an elder handed out copies of the map showing the village with hand-drawn assigned areas that each group would search.

***

Mary and Augusto boarded the six thirty-two a.m. train to Paris through Poitiers. They relaxed a little as they sat down opposite each other so that they could have opposing views of the aisle.

"Where are we heading when we arrive in Paris?" Augusto asked.

"I really do not know. The first thing is to find a library to try to contact someone in the United States who will be very worried about me."

"Who?"

"I'd rather not say. Apparently, he could be put in danger if he is associated with me."

Augusto shifted in the chair at the word *danger*.

She knew he was unaware of the last few days' events, and she did not want to give any more information than was necessary to keep him safe.

"I have a cousin in Paris who may be able to help us. He does have some mental health issues," Augusto said. "He is a little off, and if we meet him, please just ignore his outbursts. I know he has many connections and will be a good contact. The other thing is that he speaks English."

"Off?"

"Yes, I mean *really* out there. His name is Gustave. We can take the Paris RER to his *arrondissement*."

"The what to his what?" Mary asked.

"Oh, sorry ... Subway to his neighborhood."

"Okay, let's meet with him."

"How did you learn English?" Mary asked, wanting to use the remaining time on the train to learn more about Augusto.

"I was born in Japan, and my parents placed me in an English-speaking Catholic school. I was taught in English until we moved."

"How old were you then?"

"Eight."

"What do you like to do?"

"Read. I love the classics," he said, smiling. "It was my only escape from life at the monastery growing up."

"I see."

He leaned in. "When I was younger, I dreamed of becoming a writer. I have been praying to God to be blessed with talent. Now I write short stories and poems, mostly."

"Oh, really? I love poetry. Would you be so kind as to share one with me?"

"I don't know," he said, glancing at his burlap sack on the seat next to him.

"Please?" Mary pleaded.

"Okay."

Augusto reached into his sack and pulled out a tattered notebook. "I hope it doesn't smell like cheese," he said jokingly.

Mary did not get the joke, but she laughed politely.

Augusto leafed through the book, turning pages. Finally, he stopped and cleared his throat. "No, it's too painful," he said, slamming the book closed.

Startled, Mary reached out and grabbed his hand. Maybe what he had written brought back sad memories.

He looked up at Mary with tears in his eyes. "Thank you."

"Not a problem. When you're ready—no rush."

Augusto placed the tattered notebook back in the burlap sack, sat back, and closed his eyes. He looked tired.

"Go ahead and rest, Augusto. I will take first watch and wake you, if needs be."

"Okay," Augusto said, keeping his eyes closed.

Mary pulled out her phone to check her text messages. Many were from her dad, pleading for her to return to the monastery. She hit the *delete* button over and over again until she reached a text from Maxwell.

Mary, I am coming to find you. Send a location of where you are. Desperate. <sad face emoji>

She felt knots form in the pit of her stomach. "No, no, Maxwell," she said, the words slipping out of her mouth.

She noticed Augusto quickly open one eye then close it.

This is bad, really bad ... He will be in such danger! She wanted to text him and tell him that she was okay. She wanted to tell him not to come and find her, that she loved him, but she refrained. It was too risky and would put them all in danger.

Chapter 19

PARIS

The train pulled into the Paris station. Mary and Augusto disembarked quickly and dashed into a side street.

"How far does Gustave live from the station?" Mary asked.

"I gave you the address I last remember," Augusto said. "Please, look at your phone. I do not think we need to take a subway."

Mary looked at her phone. The walking time was five minutes.

When they arrived at the apartment building, Augusto entered the hall, found Gustave's name on the board, and pressed the call button.

"*Bonjour,*" came a voice from the other end.

"*Bonjour,* Gustave, *c'est ton* cousin Augusto?"

"*Qui?*"

"Augusto."

"Ah, Augusto, *tu fais ici?*"

"*Je suis avec une madame.*"

The call ended abruptly and, in a flash, Gustave was standing in front of them. He was a heavy-set man, about twenty-five years old, with hazel eyes and uncombed brown hair nestled under a beret. His handlebar mustache was oiled to the tips and framed by a day-old beard.

"*Mademoiselle*, a pleasure to meet you," Gustave said in broken English. He reached to grab her hand for a kiss.

Augusto slapped his hand down. "No, Gustave, she is a special *mademoiselle*."

"*Sienna, brulee!*" Gustave shouted out. Then he motioned for them both to follow him up the stairs. As they did, Gustave shouted, "*Blue cerulean!*"

"What is he saying?" Mary whispered.

"*Vert viridien*. Colors of his palette. He shouts out colors of paints all day long. It's his curse from having too many concussions from playing football when he was younger. He is a brilliant artist, though. Wait until you see his work."

Gustave knocked then opened his apartment door. "Please, come in. Would you like some tea or coffee?" He then asked a mannequin that was sitting at a small kitchen table to boil water and make some tea. "This is Genevieve. She says Augusto owes me money." He laughed. "Say hi to our guests, Genevieve." He waited a minute. "Rude, as always."

"Sure, I will have tea. Thank you, Gustave," Mary said, giggling.

Mary looked around the apartment in awe. There were hundreds of pieces of artwork; some leaning against the walls, others layered on furniture and tables. Most were landscapes, all brightly colored and executed masterfully. A strong smell of linseed oil filled the air.

"I absolutely love your work," Mary said, walking slowly through the rooms.

"Oh, thank you very much. I dabble in the arts," he said before shouting, "*Orange brulee!*"

"You have such a wide talent," she said. "It seems that you can paint all styles very well. Do you show your work often?"

"Thank you, but unfortunately, never. It is difficult to sell my work with this condition that people do not understand—*Blue outremer!* This market will not give me the time of day, just looks of pity, so they pile up here and surround Genevieve and me!"

Mary gave Augusto a look.

"Let's take a photo of you. No one is going to believe that such a beautiful woman is in my apartment." Gustave fumbled through his pocket to pull out his phone.

Mary and Augusto walked over to the window, and Gustave took a photo. He then asked Augusto to move over, and move over some more, until Mary thought he was out of the frame.

"I do not think I am in the photo," Augusto said.

"Cousin, I grew up with you; why do I need a photo of you to remember you by? *La mademoiselle est aussi belle qu'un champ de lys blancs dansant au vent!*"

"Gustave, we need your help," Augusto said. "My friend here needs to get back to the United States as soon as possible."

"*Shh* ... Augusto! I am in a modeling session."

"Oh my God!" Augusto said, sitting down opposite Genevieve at the table.

After taking his photos, Gustave said he had a friend in the air cargo business that subcontracts for UPS. He used his phone to contact him then spent the next few minutes texting back and forth.

"Good news ... *Blanc de titane* ... He is leaving for Melbourne, Australia tonight, and he says that people do catch rides with him to places for no-frills, inexpensive airfare."

"How is that good news?" Augusto asked. "Melbourne is quite far from the States."

"It's inexpensive, and they speak English," Gustave said with a smile. "Let me know. He is waiting for an answer."

Mary and Augusto looked at each other.

"Well, it would put us farther from the situation and the bores," Mary said.

"Yes," Augusto agreed. "How much is it, Gustave?"

"Forty-five and fifty-nine Francs, or fifty U.S. for both ... cousin rate," he said proudly.

"Let's go then," Mary replied.

"Super!" Gustave said. "I will take you to the airport in my new Citroën Ami in a few hours."

Mary wanted to get some rest, so Gustave cleared a space on the couch where she could lie down. She could hear Augusto and Gustave talking in French and laughing in the other room.

Family is everything, she thought as she drifted off to sleep.

***

"Time to go, Mary," Augusto said as he stood above her with her knapsack in hand.

They left the apartment and walked downstairs to a vehicle parked in front of the building. It was tiny and pastel green, and it looked to fit only two passengers.

Augusto looked at Gustave. "That is your car?"

"Yes. Isn't it cute? Artist budget," he said, smiling.

Augusto took what seemed like forever trying to cram himself into the passenger seat. Finally, he settled in, putting the seat all the way back and asked Mary to sit on his lap. She hesitated but did so. It was the only option.

Gustave started down the road, and Mary looked out the small passenger-side window, watching the people pass.

"What the freak!" she exclaimed. She turned around to look out the rear window for a better view.

"What, Mary, what?" Augusto asked.

"I just saw two women walking near the apartment building in royal blue cloaks, just like the one laid out for me in the monastery. I have it in my bag."

"I know a little about the royal blue cloaks," Augusto said. "Gustave, can you speed up?"

"Uh … Sorry, this beauty's top speed is a cool twenty-eight miles per hour. It's electric."

"You're kidding, right?" Augusto asked.

"No, I am trying to become more green—*vert phtalo*—and reduce my carbon footprint. I am not going to be responsible for the demise of humans, small dogs, and hedgehogs. Hedgehogs are our future."

"What?" Augusto exclaimed.

"I am hopeful that we make it there on this charge with all the extra weight … Do you have legalized pot in the United States? I love pot!"

Augusto gave Gustave a disapproving glance.

"Please, forgive me, cousin," Gustave said, "but God created pot."

"It will be okay, Mary. I am with you," Augusto said.

Gustave corrected him. "*We* are—*rouge de candium*—with you."

The Ami crawled along the highway, heading to the Airport-Le Bourget. Vehicles passed them on the left and right, honking as they sped by. Gustave did not seem to notice or mind.

"I am going to travel and paint the United States someday, and hang out with Elon Musk in Texas to talk about electric cars … and then smoke a lot of pot … not with Elon. I mean, with the many artists I expect to meet … Take a toke, paint a stroke … I can see it … What do you think?" Gustave asked.

Mary smiled while Augusto rolled his eyes.

Once through the security gate at the airport, they drove to the hangar where Gustave's friend was waiting with another pilot. The plane was huge and dwarfed the Ami.

Gustave got out and eagerly shook his friend's hand. "Thank you, Pierre, for accepting them."

"No problem. It may be a little bumpier than they are used to, but we will get them there. Come on, Gustave's friends!" Pierre motioned for Mary and Augusto to follow him as he turned to climb the ladder to the plane.

Mary shook Gustave's hand. "Thank you very much for your help, Gustave."

A jolt of electricity shot through Gustave's body and ended with a split-second of intense shooting pain in his head. He winced and immediately felt odd. Stunned, he then said a slow goodbye and stood there for a few minutes before he got into the Ami, waved, and drove off.

He noticed that he did not shout one paint color the entire ride home. His good fortune continued over the next few hours, and he was growing more and more excited that he had just experienced some sort of miracle from Mary's touch.

He took out his Bible and prayed until bedtime.

***

On the plane, Mary and Augusto walked by large crates and boxes on wrapped pallets. There was a small cabin near the front of the aircraft, with the two pilot seats and, behind them, two bathrooms and six additional seats for passengers. Mary and Augusto sat down and buckled up.

"*Monsieur* and *Madame*, we have water and snacks in the cooler that you can access once we reach thirty thousand feet. Sorry there are no frills on this plane. And I also just want to warn you it may be a bumpy ride due to an unsettled weather system."

The plane took off and ascended quickly into the darkness. Mary took out a book that she had recycled from Gustave and started to read. Augusto took out his tattered notebook and began to write. All was well for now.

***

The plane jolted violently and dropped, jarring Augusto awake. He screamed and looked at Mary, who was composed and, although startled, gave him a reassuring look.

The plane dropped again, this time farther, and felt as if it would crack apart. Augusto grabbed Mary's hand. He immediately felt the fear leave him.

"*Uh ... Sorry, folks, that was a very bad downdraft,*" Pierre said over the loudspeaker. "*We fell about seven thousand feet in seconds. We do not expect any more of those.*"

"Everything will be okay," Mary said.

Augusto continued to hold Mary's hand, and she could feel his heartbeat and breathing slow.

She had no fear, just an overwhelming feeling of peace. She was beginning to believe that she might be as special as everyone claimed her to be.

Chapter 20

TRENDING

The next day, Gustave woke and, to his amazement, did not recite any colors for hours. He decided to place the photo of Mary and his story on social media, realizing that this was something extraordinary. Gustave was oblivious of the threat to everyone that hitting the *enter* button would cause. He titled the post "Man Healed by Woman Named Mary" and, at midday, the post began to go viral. His account exploded with inquiries about where he lived and who Mary was. He did not reply to any of the comments, as he knew that Mary was running from something and failed to connect that the *something* was soon going to be on its way to find him.

***

The post now was rapidly being viewed worldwide as the plane landed in Melbourne the next morning and taxied to the UPS hanger.

Mary and Maxwell climbed down the ladder and walked across the tarmac.

"We need to get downtown to see if they have a library and hostel, or somewhere cheap we can stay," Mary said. "We are running out of money."

They went through the terminal and spotted a line of taxis, successfully securing one.

Mary was able to find an inexpensive hostel called Space Hotel on the way and gave the driver the directions. The place had an internet café. She was excited to try to contact Maxwell.

The cab pulled up to the hostel, and Mary and Augusto entered the lobby. It was much nicer than she had expected for the twenty dollar rate. There was even a bar and movie theater. This was the perfect spot to lay low for a few days until they could figure out how to travel to the States.

There were many people around who were close to their age, walking about and enjoying themselves. She yearned to be in their position.

As they walked to their room, Mary noticed a few people staring at her. She thought she heard one girl even say her name, but that would be impossible.

Mary and Augusto stayed in their room for a few hours.

"I am going to do a load of laundry. Will you give me all your clothes, including your tunic, so that I can wash them? You may want to shower, also, while we have the chance," Mary said.

After she returned from the laundry room, she went to take a shower. Soon after that, she returned and settled in to read. Augusto showered next, and upon his return, he pulled out his tattered notebook.

He looked at Mary. "Okay, I am ready."

"Ready for what?"

"To read you one of my poems."

"Brilliant. Please, do." Mary placed her book on the nightstand, took off her glasses, and laid them beside it. She then lay back in the bed and closed her eyes. "Okay, I am ready to listen. You have all of my attention." She giggled.

"No laughing."

"I won't. I promise."

Augusto opened the notebook and began to read. "This one is called *Wild Dawn* …

> *"First light,*
> *A morning shower shatters the eerie stillness.*
> *The fusty odor of a dampened forest floor lingers.*
> *Dawn.*
> *Morning chill,*
> *Penetrates my flimsy dwelling of canvas and strings.*
> *An open fire hampered by a young day's moods.*
> *Dawn.*
> *It has ceased.*
> *Water droplets beat unsynchronized rhythms.*
> *This diminishing world is slowly drying up.*
> *Dawn."*

Augusto looked up proudly.

Mary lay there silently, and after a few seconds, she could only say, "Wow." There was a lump in her throat.

"Well?" he asked.

"Augusto, I don't know how to put this so it will be believable, but that poem was one of the best poems I have ever bloody heard."

"Thanks, but you are just saying that."

"No! As you were reading in that voice, I could see it, hear it, and smell it like I was there, like I was living it. I mean, I am super impressed. Where did you learn to write like that?"

"I had lots of time while living in the cellar."

"Wait—what? You lived in a freaking cellar?"

"Not lived—*live*. I have been sort of banished and confined to the lower cellar in the abbey since we moved to France. I live among the curing meats, aging cheeses, cold, mold, and the occasional mouse."

"That is why you made the cheese jokes?"

"Yes."

Mary could feel anger building up inside her. She could not believe what she was hearing. How could they confine a brother monk to a cellar?

"I need to take a walk," she said. "Let's venture around the city. There is a green nearby that I saw on the lobby map."

They left the room, walked through the lobby, and onto Russell Street to La Trobe Street. At the end of La Trobe, they entered Colton Gardens as the sun was setting. The city was beautiful in the light, and people were out enjoying the evening weather.

A couple speaking in an unfamiliar language walked by, and Mary listened to the conversation as it faded behind her. She was amazed that she could almost understand what they were saying.

That is so odd, she thought to herself. *Am I imagining this? I only know English and some Spanish. How can I know what they were saying? Is it a mind trick from stress?*

She shrugged it off and kept walking.

Her phone dinged, and she looked at it quickly to read the text. It was sent from an unfamiliar number.

Scimus qui sis. Numquam succedent.

Mary stopped walking. "What the hell? Augusto, can you read this text?"

"Sure, it says, '*We know who you are. You will never succeed.*'"

Mary put the phone down slowly and did not say much. It was difficult to understand why someone would send such a cryptic, hateful message.

"Succeed at what …? I do not know what or who this text is referring to. I really do not understand this message. It sounds like a threat, and I am growing more and more concerned."

Mary remembered what Dr. Strum had said about the Collective and regained a little more confidence. She looked around, seeing there were people nearby.

"Let's keep walking, Augusto, but please stay close."

Chapter 21

HEAVEN SENT

They walked toward the Melbourne Museum in the center of the green, and Mary noticed a woman pushing a stroller approaching. As she neared, the woman stopped and took a photo of them. Mary heard the distinct *click* of an iPhone shutter. She then grabbed the baby out of the stroller and ran toward them.

"Augusto," Mary said nervously as the woman drew closer.

"Mary, Mary, my baby is sick with cancer. Can you heal her like you did that guy in France? Please, Mary, I will devote much more of my time to God if you can heal her."

Mary cowered behind Augusto. "What guy? Who are you? And what are you saying?" Mary asked. "Please, carry on."

"Yes, please, lady, carry on," Augusto said. "We do not know what you are talking about. You must have mistaken her with someone else."

They walked past her, quickening their pace.

The woman grew defensive and followed. "You are the Mary in the post about a guy who could not help himself from saying paint colors all day. I am not crazy. He had mental health issues from too many concussions or something, and after you touched him, he was healed of his illness."

Stunned, Mary stopped and faced the woman. "How do you know that?"

"The post on social media, it has gone viral," the woman said, lowering her voice. "You have no idea, do you?"

"No. Listen, I do not have any healing powers. That guy must have fabricated the story to increase his popularity."

"So, you will not heal my baby, Aurora? You will not even try?" The woman started to cry.

"Sorry, lady, I cannot help you," Mary said. "I am really, really sorry. I am not the one."

They continued to walk away, but then Mary stopped, remembering the photo that the woman had taken of them earlier. It could pose a risk.

She walked back to where the lady still stood. "You delete the photo you took of us earlier, and I will place my hand on the baby's forehead to wish her well. Agreed?"

"Agreed."

"What kind of cancer does she have?" Mary asked.

"They found an inoperable tumor in her brain," the woman said, sobbing.

Mary took the baby from the woman's arms and gently placed her hand on her forehead. She was precious, and all Mary felt was love for her. She was surprised that the feeling was so intense and connected, as if she knew her. She said a prayer then handed the baby back.

"The photo?"

"Oh, right." The woman reached into her pocket to grab her phone. She deleted the photo.

"Goodbye, precious one," Mary said. "Take care of her."

"Thank you, thank you, thank you!"

As Mary turned toward Augusto, she realized a crowd had gathered. Augusto's size and the robes that they were wearing made them a curiosity, and the commotion with the woman had attracted attention.

"Mary, can you touch my husband's hand, also?" a woman asked, pulling her husband's hand toward her.

"I cannot. I am sorry."

Mary quickly pulled on the hood of her cloak. "Let's find a bar. I need a drink," she said as they quickly continued down the path and out of the park.

She pulled the hood of the cloak tighter over her head and put on a pair of sunglasses that she had pulled from her purse. "I look discreet but, Augusto, you stand out like a holy mountain with a burning bush beaconing *come find me*!" she said, trying to lighten the mood. "Do you think Gustave would have done that? Post a photo of me on the web?"

"He must have. How else would the woman know your name and about Gustave's illness?"

***

The doctor walked into the exam room with an expression of disbelief.

He looked at the films again and shook his head. "I don't know how to tell you this, but we are witnesses to a miracle of God," he said. "The scans indicate that there is no tumor in Aurora's brain anymore, not even the residual evidence of one. There is no medical explanation, and—"

The woman fainted and collapsed. The doctor dropped the films and lunged toward her to break her fall.

"Nurse, nurse!" he called out, and two nurses came running in. They pulled a chair over to the unconscious woman and sat her in it. When they revived her, she looked up.

"Is this a dream?" she asked softly.

"No, you passed out," the doctor said. "We were discussing that your baby is healed."

"Healed?" The woman looked toward Aurora, sleeping in the stroller.

"Yes, completely healed—there is no more cancer. I can't explain it."

"It was Mary. It must have been Mary."

"Say again?"

"A beautiful woman named Mary, sent from heaven. I met her in the park." Tears streamed down her face.

"I see. Very well then. Enjoy the rest of the year. I will see you in six months," the doctor instructed in his usual clinical speech.

The woman collected her things and stepped out in the street. She smiled to herself as she frantically dialed her husband to share the news. She knew she had been the recipient of something miraculous and had met someone for whom the world had been waiting for, for over two thousand years.

Chapter 22

GOD BLESS

Maxwell and Mattea stepped off the plane in Paris. There was a vehicle with a small cross on the door, waiting to pick them up outside of baggage claim.

"Welcome, Mattea! I see you have a good-looking friend traveling with you," the driver said as she placed their baggage in the trunk. She then turned to Maxwell. "Hi, I am Sister Anna, and you are?"

"Maxwell."

"Nice to meet you, *Monsieur* Maxwell." Her English flowed with a French accent. Her perfect ebony skin radiated her beauty. "The abbess Isabella Maria Barachie wants to meet you right away once you arrive at the school."

They rode to the convent on narrow streets. Maxwell marveled at the architecture and the ages of the homes as they passed. They soon arrived at the convent, and Sister Anna opened the car door for them.

"Please, follow me," she said.

They walked down a long corridor to a room where the abbess was waiting for them, seated behind a large wooden desk. Two nuns were seated on a couch to her right with pen and paper in hand. A muted sunlight broke through the window, struggling to illuminate the gloom.

"I am glad you are here, Mattea. You look well," the abbess said as she stood up and walked around the desk to give Mattea a firm hug. "It's been too long, my good friend. And unfortunately, we have quite a serious situation."

"Serious?" Maxwell asked. "What kind of situation?"

"You must be *Monsieur* Maxwell, the boyfriend ... I am happy to meet you," the abbess said as she sat back down in her chair.

"I heard a little about it from other members, and thank you for sending me the message about Paris," Mattea said. "Otherwise, we would have headed to London to begin our search."

"I am sure you have heard that Abbot San Frisco has lost her ... or, rather, allowed her to leave the monastery grounds. Do you believe that someone so important, so revered, who we have been looking for, for centuries, is now at risk due to his complacency turned carelessness? I had no choice but to call for the activation of the entire European Collective and place the America Collective on standby. It is only a matter of time before she is located. She has no idea the danger she is in. I have the sisterhood scouring this continent." Upset, the abbess words became louder and louder as she spoke.

Maxwell grew more and more nervous hearing the gravity of the situation. He did not know what to do. What made Mary so special? And, why had she left the monastery? He had an impending urge to look for her and stood up to leave.

"Where are you going, young man?" Isabella asked.

"We need to do something. We need to be out there if Mary is in danger. What kind of danger, I do not know, but I love this woman, and I am going to look for her."

"I see," Isabella said as she took out a cigarette from the side drawer and lit it. "Love is a very strong word. Do you even know who you are in love with?"

"Yes," Maxwell said, feeling panicked. "Mary, the one who can see."

Isabella dropped her cigarette on the floor and started coughing uncontrollably.

"What did you say?" Mattea asked.

"Mary, my girlfriend, is the one who can see."

Trying to regain her composure, she took a few deep breaths and dismissed the two nuns, walked over to the door, and shut it.

"Maxwell, how do you know this?" she asked. "What does she see?"

"Unimportant. I am leaving to try to find her." Maxwell knew Mary better than anyone in this room and had given them too much information already. He needed to start searching.

Isabella, reading his defensive body language, thought it wise not to push him or prolong the meeting any longer. She realized that she needed to know how and why he knew what he did. Mattea was her connection.

"You must stay by Mattea's side at all times. This country is foreign to you, and so is the language. Besides, you are also in danger. If captured, you will be made a pawn. I cannot express to you the seriousness of this situation."

She turned to Mattea. "You are now assigned as his protector."

"Yes, Mother Superior," Mattea said.

"Captured? Situation? Pawn? What are you talking about?" Maxwell asked. "I am just a college student from New York. Who is after Mary?"

"They are known as The Order, an organization that split from the church thousands of years ago. For generations, they have tried to force their beliefs on the world's populations. They do not believe in coexisting; it's their way *only*. They are pinned by evil. After centuries, we are still stuck in our ideals, compassion is waning, and the world is unwell. It is almost like the days of Saladin and the Knights Templar—archenemies. Nothing will be accomplished with humanity divided. Heed my warning. God bless you. Now, please, go find Mary."

Chapter 23

THUD

Mattea and Maxwell left the convent and walked out of the gate to the street. He had no idea where he was going or where to start. He was lost and confused until his phoned dinged, announcing a new email. One of his friends had sent him a post from a man in Paris with the words, "*This looks like your girlfriend. It's viral.*"

Maxwell opened the link, looked at the photo, and gasped. It was unmistakable. It was Mary! He could not believe it.

"Mattea, she's in Paris, she's in Paris! Let's go!" He started running down the street in his excitement until he realized he had no idea where he was going.

"Let me see," Mattea said, catching up to him.

Maxwell showed her the phone and replayed the post.

"Are you sure it's her?" she asked.

He showed her other photos on his phone that he had taken of Mary.

"Yes, that's her. Let's go to the train station and catch a train to Paris immediately. It's the quickest way." Mattea led him down a narrow, house-lined street.

They did not walk far when a vehicle approached them from behind. Maxwell heard the whining engine of speed as it closed in, and he turned around just in time for Mattea to push him up against a wall. He then heard a sickening *thud* and muted cracking as he watched Mattea fly into the air and over the vehicle. She landed in the street, facedown, staring ahead with one eye open as blood seeped onto the cobblestone from a head wound, her legs laying in unnatural angles. He stared at her in horror as her mouth seemed to form words without sound. Then her one blood-filled eye shifted and looked directly at him.

"Run!" she shouted.

Maxwell panicked and began to run down the street. He could hear the squealing of tires as the culprit made quick turns on the streets behind him. He couldn't believe what he had just seen. The brutality of it.

As he distanced himself from the scene, he heard sirens filling the air and growing louder, knowing they were for Mattea. He ran, looking in both directions, up and down the passing streets, until he saw the icon for a train. He followed the sign's arrow and soon arrived at a train station.

He ran inside and up to the window. He tried to ask for a ticket to Paris, but he was breathing too hard to get the words out. The agent kept asking him the same question in French, not understanding. Maxwell was growing panicked. He could feel himself sweating and his heart racing. A young man approached him.

"Hello. May I offer my assistance?" he said in English.

"Yes, I am trying to get to Paris, and the agent keeps asking me the same question. I don't understand French." Maxwell's voice was quivery.

The young man spoke to the agent in French then motioned for Maxwell to hand him the money. The agent handed him a ticket.

"I am traveling to Paris with my girl. You can accompany us, if you'd like. We can help you with the language barrier."

"Sure, that would be nice," Maxwell said slowly, although he wasn't feeling quite right.

"My name is Robert Bracco. I am from the States."

"I am Maxwell. New York."

Maxwell was in a daze. Everyone seemed to speak and move slowly. He felt as if he was going to pass out as he made his way to the nearest empty bench. Robert sat down next to him.

"I need water," Maxwell said.

Robert handed him a bottle of water from his knapsack. "What happened to you, man? You don't look too good."

"I just witnessed a very bad accident, and someone was really hurt," Maxwell said, choking up.

"Oh, that's too bad, bro," Robert said. "The water is yours."

A woman approached them and sat down next to Robert.

"This is my girl, Carol-Anne."

"Nice you meet ... I mean, nice to meet you," Maxwell said, barely able to turn his head to look at her.

An announcement soon came over the loudspeaker. "*Le train pour la France débarquera à partir du quai un.*"

A few minutes later, the train to Paris pulled into the station.

"This is us," Robert said as he and his girlfriend got up from their seats, but Maxwell did not move. He felt as if he needed to throw up. "Are you with us?"

The feeling passed.

"Sure," he said as he stood up and grabbed his bag, knowing his options were limited.

They boarded the train and sat down together. Soon, they were on their way.

Maxwell was desperate to find Mary. He had no way to contact the abbess, nor would he want to try after what had just happened.

That car was targeting us, he thought, terrified and in shock, as he stared out the window. He did not know who had been behind it.

Chapter 24

MATTEA

The phone rang on the abbess's desk, and she answered it promptly.

"*Bonjour.*"

"*Bonjour, madame,* do you speak English?"

"Yes."

"This is Dr. Lucas Mathieu, calling from the Poitiers University Hospital. *Madame,* I regret to inform you that we believe one of your sisters was brought in badly hurt. We did everything we could to save her, but she did not make it. We need someone to come down to the hospital and identify the body."

"*Quelle?*"

"*Madame,* one of your sisters has died in a tragic car accident. Actually, one witness described it as a hit and run."

The abbess was silent as tears welled up in her eyes. She knew who it could be.

"What was she wearing?" she asked, not really wanting to know the answer.

"A royal blue cloak with silver trim and a silver *C* pin with a cross in it. The cloak was clasped with a second larger, silver cross. Inside the cloak, the name Mattea is embroidered."

"Is there a young man, also?"

"No."

"I will be right over," she said, her voice cracking.

Isabella hung up the phone, reached into the side drawer, pulled out a cigarette, and placed it between her lips. She lit the match, and the flame brightened the gloom of the room for a few brief seconds. Her hand was shaking.

She sat there, taking drag after drag, silently praying for Mattea while smoking the cigarette to the butt then lit another one. She knew this was going to be one of the most difficult things she had ever done. She had seen hundreds of dead people before and saved thousands of souls, but this one was different. This was one of her sisters, a high-ranking protector in the Collective, loved by all and taken by an evil act. This was her best childhood friend.

It figures they would have used a vehicle as they would have had a tough time in hand-to-hand combat with her, Isabella thought to herself.

Mattea had been one of the best. Delivered to the convent as an orphan when she had only been ten years old, she had trained incessantly, every day, to become the ultimate protector.

The abbess snuffed out the cigarette in an ashtray that was rapidly filling with butts then slowly rose from her chair. She took a deep breath, walked over to her royal blue cloak trimmed with gold hanging on the rack, and laid it across her arm. She then opened the office door and asked the sister guarding the hall to call for a car.

***

Isabella arrived at the hospital and forced herself to walk in. She was happy she had asked two elder sisters to accompany her for support.

"This is so maddening! Why would God take her? I don't understand. She was so good, so devoted. She was my sister.

She was my best friend. She was a gift from God," she said as they walked into the building.

The doctor met them at the front desk and asked only one of them to follow.

"Wait here in the lobby, please," the abbess said to the two sisters.

The two walked down the hall to the morgue. Isabella paused and took a deep breath before entering.

The room was filled with stainless steel tables, and on a few were black bags laid out. The doctor walked to one and stopped.

"I am so sorry you have to do this. I wish this could be different," he said before he unzipped the body bag.

The abbess gasped.

It was Mattea's face, disfigured and bruised.

Isabella placed her hand over her mouth, trying to keep her composure the best she could. "Yes, it is our sister, Mattea Sinclair, from the United Kingdom," she told her doctor, her voice shaking.

"I am so sorry for your loss. Please, follow me, and I will give you the belongings that she came in with."

The doctor led her back to the lobby, and as she spoke to the two sisters, he handed her the cross clasp and silver *C* pin that Mattea had worn.

"What would you like us to do with the cloak?" he asked. "It is quite damaged."

"Please, dispose of it," the abbess said as she and the sisters walked out of the building, crying.

Chapter 25

NIGHTMARE

Mary did not sleep well. She had nightmares of a pandemic that killed thousands of people, of divided populations, protests, and even riots, and a catastrophic asteroid strike that wiped out part of a continent. She tossed, turned, and woke up upset and sweating, her heart beating quickly.

"How did you sleep?" Augusto asked, yawning. He sat up in his bed, which was way too short for him, his feet dangling off the end.

"Not well. I had terrible nightmares."

"Can I ask what about? I have an interest in people's nightmares."

She sat up and rubbed her eyes. "It was strange. So realistic." She looked at him. "That's an odd interest. Let's find some coffee downstairs, and then I will tell you."

"Sounds good," Augusto said, getting out of bed and putting on his shoes.

They went down to a little nook that contained coffee, tea, and crumpets. Mary poured two cups of coffee, and then they walked outside to the rooftop deck area to sit in the morning sun. It was already warming up.

They spoke about what they thought the next move should be to try to catch a ride to the States. Low on money, Mary was going to try to find an ATM machine. She knew her dad would be monitoring her account, but they had to eat and find a way home.

"Well, tell me about the nightmares," Augusto said.

"Are you sure you want to hear?" She took a sip of her coffee. "You know, I healed Gustave with my touch," she said jokingly. She looked off toward the Melbourne skyline. "In less than a year, there will be a pandemic that originates in Asia and spreads throughout the world, killing hundreds of thousands of people. The world governments will cooperate in developing a vaccine to beat it, but it divides the populations. There are riots and protests. In three hundred years' time, there will be an asteroid strike that will wipe out twenty-five percent of a continent. I do not know which one. Before the strike, the world governments will cooperate to build a spacecraft called Earth Arks that will be used to collect DNA and species of animals and plants on every continent that will be sent to the colonies on the moon and the few already established on Mars. We will also build immense underground DNA and cryogenic species banks run by only computers and robots, so they can repopulate the Earth following the catastrophic event. Elon Musk's SpaceX is successful ... That's fantastic, huh?"

"I guess so," Augusto said.

Mary continued, "The superpowers and countries of the world will realize the politics that they are spending time on now, and the posturing, is all trivial compared to the real threats that humanity will face. They are arguing and fighting amongst themselves for fire and dust ... for fire and dust ..." Her voice faded as she looked down at the ground, trying to recall the visions.

Finally, Augusto spoke, "Wow, how depressing! Sounds more like visions than nightmares. You know I really do not like any bad news, especially news where Earth gets destroyed."

Mary noticed that Augusto was slightly rocking back and forth. "Hey, it's okay, Augusto."

"Would you like a crumpet?" Augusto reached for one. "I love saying the word *crumpet*. It is so neat."

"I don't know what it was, but it was very upsetting. It is so tragic that, in the future, we will need to find a new planet to save the species on this one, recognizing the inevitable truth that one day an asteroid will hit Earth, as they have for millions of years. Elon Musk must know. That could be one of the reasons he founded SpaceX."

"What about that new agency in the United States? What is it called? Space Force? Don't they have an asteroid defense system?"

"No idea. But I hope so. Anyway, I told you the nightmares were strange. It was very hard to sleep."

"I guess the world population should repent and confess," Augusto said.

"Probably." Mary did not want to dwell on the subject. "Okay, we need to locate an ATM far from this area."

Once they finished eating, they walked downstairs and out of the hotel. Mary decided to head to the waterfront to find an ATM. It was a long walk in the heat with her cloak and hood pulled up, but she had to conceal herself. She noticed people looking at them strangely, but none of them approached. They ended up on the Bay Trail and eventually found an ATM near a busy café called Rock, Paper, Scissors.

"We need to keep moving," she said after she withdrew the money. She checked the status of her VPN and made a mental note to return to the café someday; she liked the feel of it. "They all could know we are in Melbourne by now. We need to leave soon."

A group of three men in dark suits approached them. Mary worried that they could be with the bores, but they passed.

She thought about her dad and how worried he must be, but she also thought about the three nuns killed in the accident and how everyone seemed to be at risk around her.

A kid stopped in front of Augusto, blocking his path. "Are you the monk in *The Avengers*?" he asked.

"Sorry, kid. No, I am not."

"Boy, you are big. I bet you can beat up the Hulk."

"No, not a chance."

The kid looked him up and down. "I agree; not a chance," he said then continued on his way.

Chapter 26

FTWS

Maxwell arrived in Paris with Robert and Carol-Anne and decided to stick with them. He debated whether to tell them about his search for Mary.

"Hey, where are you guys heading?"

"Well, we want to see the Eiffel Tower and the Louvre, eat some local foods, and try to get rudely yelled at by a Parisian, you know, for the whole experience. Other than that, we are open. Do you have any ideas?"

"None," Maxwell responded. "I am looking for a friend, and she is supposed to be in the city somewhere."

"Nice. Where?"

"I do not know."

"I say you hang with us until you figure it out, bro. You look like you could use some friends."

"Sure, but I want to find a hotel. I am still shaken up. It was a very upsetting morning."

They spent the rest of the day touring the city and looking for a place to stay.

Maxwell was mundane. He thought about Mattea and the crash constantly, especially the sounds of it and how she had sacrificed herself to save him. He did not want to damper

Robert's and Carol-Anne's experience any further, so he decided to leave them to book two rooms at the Hilton Paris Opera.

He arrived at the hotel midafternoon. As he walked to the elevator, he noticed the Le Grand Salon. It was exceptional; majestically decorated in a Napoleonic style.

Once in his room, he decided to sit down and see if he had any messages on his phone that would give him a better idea of where Mary could be. To his surprise, he had received an email from an unknown address. He almost deleted it, thinking it was spam, but then he saw letters *FTWS* in the subject line, and there was a photo attached. He was desperate for information.

Here goes nothing, he thought as he clicked on the link to download.

It was a photo of Newport Tower. Mary must have sent it. FTWS stood for *For Those Who See.* He zoomed into the photo for a closer look.

His eyes focused on small letters drawn among the stones. They were barely visible. He walked over to the desk and started to write them down.

U M L B A O N R S E U E

He did not know what to make of them. Maybe it was a puzzle? He rearranged them again and again and finally came up with *MELBOURNE*, plus three letters. *AUS.*

"That's it!" he said excitedly. *She must be in Melbourne, Australia!*

He called the airport to see what flights were available in the morning. He found an early one and booked it.

***

Mary stood up from the computer desk, took another bite of her sandwich, and then left after sending Maxwell a second photo of the map of Newport with letters barely circled in the name of streets. She placed a tiny dot in the circle near the letter on the ones that she wanted Maxwell to notice. She knew that Maxwell would be able to decipher her messages.

She did not want to have him near her, but she decided that she needed him now more than ever.

***

The next morning, Maxwell grabbed a pen and notepad on the nightstand and began to write:

Robert and Carol-Anne,

I had to leave unexpectedly. Thank you for your help and friendship. I will always remember it. Stay safe.

Best,

Maxwell Downs

He slipped the note under their room door then left. He walked past the desk and let the maître d' and receptionists know that they were to take good care of his guests in room 529.

Chapter 27

MELBOURNE

When Maxwell's plane arrived in Melbourne, he immediately looked up the address of the hostel that Mary had provided with the road map that she had sent.

He stood on the sidewalk and tried to hail a taxi. He saw one slowing down and pulling over when another one pulled in front of it, cutting it off.

The driver rolled down the window and asked, "In need of a taxi, mate?"

"Yes."

"Sorry for my aggressive driving, but we are having taxi wars here in Melbourne."

Maxwell handed the driver his bag and got in.

"Where to?"

Maxwell showed the driver the address on his phone.

"No worries, mate."

Maxwell's excitement grew into a frenzy; he could feel his heart beating fast. This was the cumulation of the weekslong search for Mary.

Finally, after twenty minutes, the taxi stopped in front of the hostel.

Maxwell got out and paid the fare then entered the lobby and texted Mary.

Here.

He waited, nervously pacing, and soon the elevator doors opened. There, standing in front of him, was Mary. Tears filled their eyes as they ran to each other and hugged in a strong embrace. They hugged and hugged, not wanting to let each other go.

"I love you so much, Maxwell."

"I love you, too, Mary."

***

Augusto was now uncomfortably standing to the side of Mary, trying to look at anything else but their embrace. He knew that if he remained in France as a monk, he would not be permitted to find love and companionship as strong as theirs. Yet, it was something he yearned for. Eventually, he wanted to relocate back to Japan, his mom's native country. He had family there, and monks could marry after receiving their higher ordination.

Augusto cleared his throat.

"Oh, forgive me, Maxwell. This is Augusto, my protector. He has traveled with me from the monastery in France and is now a good friend."

Augusto reached out his massive hand to shake Maxwell's. "Nice to meet you, sir. I would say I heard a lot about you, but I haven't."

"Let's go get some tea, sit on the rooftop deck in the sun, and catch up," Mary said.

"Absolutely," Maxwell replied.

She grabbed Maxwell's hand and walked with him toward the coffee nook. "Sorry, they only have regular tea; no peach tea."

"Any cup of tea will do."

They took the elevator to the rooftop deck and sat down in the sun, catching each other up on their travels over the past few weeks. Maxwell was concerned about who was behind the nuns' deaths, and Mary was stunned and saddened about Mattea's horrific end.

Maxwell told them all about how his uncle had helped him and about Mattea and the abbess. Then Mary told him about her visit to London, the museum, the stay at the abbey, and the crash, even the injured calf.

After that, the conversation turned more optimistic. They talked about the sights that they had seen and the visit to Augusto's cousin, Gustave, his tiny car, and the mannequin friend, Genevieve. That was when they finally laughed.

***

Mary went back down to the coffee nook to grab some crumpets. As she approached, she heard men arguing at the reception desk. Surprisingly, one of the voices sounded familiar.

She peered around the corner, and standing there was her dad, flanked by two bores. She could not believe it! She overheard him say, "She is my daughter. I need to know what room she is in."

"Sorry, mate, we cannot divulge any information about our guests—company policy," the front desk clerk said. "You are welcome to wait in the bar for her to pass."

Mary backstepped to the elevator and quickly made her way to where Maxwell and Augusto sat. "We have to go *now*," she said, "without our things."

"But our stuff ..." Augusto said.

"We will have to get it later. My dad and the bores are in the lobby."

"What is a bore?" Maxwell asked.

"High-level security that is supposed to be protecting me, but they are failing. People died."

"Mary, you know I cannot leave without my notebook," Augusto said.

Mary thought about it then said, "Okay, we will send Maxwell down, in case they force their way up to the floor. They do not know what he looks like. This is bad. How did they find us?"

Maxwell looked down at his hands. "Probably the taxi driver. I think he was a plant. He was very aggressive."

Mary shook her head. "Take the elevator down to Room 369, on the third floor. Throw everything in my knapsack and the burlap bag that says *Café* on it then meet us back here. They cannot get up here without a key."

"Did you say burlap bag?"

"Yes. Hurry. Also, don't forget my purse; it's small and black."

Maxwell headed to the elevator and pushed the button for the third floor. When he arrived, he stepped out into the hallway and saw two men standing at the other end as he casually walked to room 369 and entered. Once inside, he threw everything that he could find in the knapsack and burlap bag. A girl and guy sat on beds, talking. They were good-looking and young, with matching sun-bleached hair, blue eyes, and tans.

"Hi, my name is Maxwell. Could you do me a favor and help me carry these items up to the rooftop deck? Have you seen it? It's quite nice."

"No, we just arrived, but sure," the guy replied as they stood up.

Maxwell handed the girl Mary's knapsack and the man the burlap bag. He then grabbed Mary's purse, gave it to the girl, and took her knapsack back as they entered the hallway. The two men still stood at the end of the hall, watching.

Finally, at the rooftop deck, they all exited the elevator.

Confused, Mary and Augusto asked who Maxwell's companions were.

"I needed help carrying your items, and these two friendly people had just arrived in the room and agreed."

"Thank you," Mary said. "What are your names?"

"John. And this is Elizabeth."

"My name is Mary."

"Hey, aren't you the woman in the video that the guy in France claimed you healed? You look just like her," Elizabeth asked Mary with her Australian accent.

Augusto glanced at Mary.

"That guy was so funny. He even did a follow-up post about some mannequin named Genna or something he lives with. I loved the part when he reenacted how he used to say the colors of his palette and how his huge cousin had to stuff himself into his tiny pastel vehicle," she said, looking up at Augusto. "And *voila*, he was healed. That tiny pastel car is bonkers," she said.

She briefly touched Mary's hand as she handed her the purse, and a burst of energy careened through Elizabeth's body. "*Ouch*," she said, pulling back. "Did you feel that?"

"Feel what?" Mary asked.

"That energy when we touched hands. It was like a supercharged static jolt."

"Sorry, no. That happens a lot when people touch me. I seem to carry a lot of static electricity." Mary rubbed her feet on the floor. What she had said was untrue, but she had no other explanation for it.

"I'd say," Elizabeth agreed, rubbing her hand.

"Let's go to the basement level and see if we can exit there. Will you two join us?" Mary asked. "My dad's here. We're trying to hide from him."

"Sure," the couple said.

As they took the stairs, Elizabeth talked in a whisper the entire way down.

"Did you happen to touch a baby in a local park here in Melbourne?"

"Why? And please, keep your voice down."

"Well, it is all over the news and in the papers. This woman saw the video from the French guy and met a woman who looked like Mary in a park. Her baby had inoperable brain cancer. She begged for Mary just to touch her baby once, which she eventually did. Later that day, she went to visit her baby's doctor for another checkup, and the scans showed the cancer was completely gone. As he was explaining this, she fainted in the doctor's arms. What a fantastic miracle!"

"Get out!" Mary exclaimed.

"Yes. Where have you been?"

They stayed in the stairwell while John looked for an exit in the basement. He found one and motioned for everyone to follow.

Once outside, they ran down a few blocks to distance themselves from the hostel.

"Thank you so much, John and Elizabeth, for your help. Unfortunately, my dad is a little much. I'd shake your hands, but I fear you may be shocked or healed from some illness," Mary said, smiling. "Can I have your emails?"

"Sure," they both said then recited them to her.

John and Elizabeth started walking back toward the hostel, but then Elizabeth turned around and said, "I knew it was you, Mary, I knew it. You healed them!"

They spent the walk back telling everyone who would listen that a savior had returned from the heavens, and her name was Mary. They spent the next few months traveling across Australia, recanting the "Miracles of Mary" to populations. The viral video soon surpassed the views of any ever posted.

Chapter 28

SYDNEY

"Let's take Maxwell to that café we saw yesterday and figure out a plan," Mary told Augusto.

"Sure."

They quickly walked back to the waterfront, went into the café, and took a seat.

"I am starving," Augusto said. "Do we have enough money for a meal?"

Mary reached into her purse, but Maxwell placed his hand on hers. "Don't worry about it. I've got it."

"You sure?"

"Yes."

The waitress arrived, and they all ordered.

"A lot of people are staring at us," Maxwell said uncomfortably.

"Yes, it seems to be a new thing, and that is why we must be in and out of here. Just be wary of someone taking a photo of us," Mary said

Augusto stood up from his chair and, in his deep, baritone voice, addressed everyone in the place. "I see many of you are staring at my friends and me here. You are correct. This is Mary from the viral video, but since it is her, she is under the protection of the church, and no one, not one of you, may approach her or take a photo of any of us. If you do, I will be forced to take your phones, or worse. You will not get them back. Now put them all away. Another thing, I am not the monk in *The Avengers*." He sat back down, gleaming.

The place erupted in motion as people tried to put their phones away and out of sight.

Mary looked up at Augusto with surprise. "What are you doing? Have you lost it?"

"The mouse has already eaten the cheese. Mary, you are becoming known worldwide."

"First, that is not a real colloquialism. It's the cat is out of the bag."

"It's lower cellar slang," Augusto said, smiling.

Mary looked around. All the customers were now minding their own business, eating and talking amongst themselves. *Wow, that worked*, she thought.

"Now, what is the best way to travel back to the United States?" she asked Augusto and Maxwell as the waitress placed their meals in front of them.

The waitress looked around then whispered to Mary, "Can I have your autograph for my two girls at home? They will not believe that you are here."

Augusto looked up at Mary, shrugged, and then returned to eating his dish.

"Sure, but it will cost you a coffee refill, please," Mary replied.

"Certainly."

Mary was careful not to touch the server while taking the pen and pad from her hands.

"This is fantastic," Augusto said between bites. "Sure beats eating thirty crumpets."

"You eat a lot of crumpets?" Maxwell asked.

"We were running low on money, so, yes, we ate a lot of free crumpets at the hostel until one day they placed a small paper sign on the tray that read, '*You ate all the crumpets.*' The word *you* was double underlined," he said, laughing. "One day, I will send them money to reimburse them for how many I ate."

Mary and Maxwell smiled.

"Do they have any cruises from here to the States?" Maxwell asked the waitress.

"Not from Melbourne, but I read that they have some from Sydney."

"How far is that?"

"Well, I drove it once with my old boyfriend, and it took us about nine hours. He turned out to be a *derro*, so we split up. He chewed tobacco and spit the entire way. Have you ever kissed a tobacco mouth?"

"You know, it's hard to find good men worthwhile of your love and respect nowadays," Mary said, winking at Maxwell.

"Oh, okay, thank you." He blushed.

"Can I borrow your phone to look up the cruises?" Maxwell asked the waitress.

"Sure," she said, taking the phone from her pocket and handing it to him.

"How about a rental car place nearby?" he asked as he started searching for cruise companies.

"Sure, there is a Thrifty not too far from here."

"Great." Maxwell handed the server back her phone, and she then left to tend to other tables.

"Here is what I am thinking," Maxwell started. "We rent a car and drive to Sydney, and then book passage on Royal Caribbean. I saw that they have a fifteen-day cruise to Hawaii. It stops in Tahiti and Bora Bora."

"Really?" Mary asked. "That is better than any flight. What about the expense?"

"I will pay for it all; don't worry. The cruise will seclude us from your dad and the bores. They probably think we would use conventional travel modes. Let us finish eating and rent a car. Agreed?"

"Agreed," Mary said.

As they walked out of the café, Augusto heard a young girl say, "Mom, he *was* in *The Avengers*," as he walked by her table.

He turned around and flexed, and the girl smiled. He then bumped his head on top of the doorjamb, and she giggled loudly.

"Hey, wait up," he said to Mary and Maxwell, rubbing his forehead as he jogged down the sidewalk.

Chapter 29

SAIL

"*This is the final boarding call. All passengers should be on board now,*" came over the loudspeaker as Mary, Maxwell, and Augusto walked down the hall to locate their suite.

"What is the name of this boat?" Augusto asked.

"Ovation of the Seas."

"What type of cabin are we staying in?"

"Let me see." Maxwell pulled out a piece of paper from his shirt pocket. "We are in a royal suite."

"Sounds nice," Augusto commented.

"Here we are—9320," Maxwell said, stopping in front of a door.

Mary opened the door and stepped in. "Wow! Maxwell, are you sure this is not the captain's quarters? This is amazing. How can you afford this?"

"Largest one on the ship for the largest man on the ship," Maxwell said. "Much deserved."

"Thank you," Augusto said.

"Well, go find your room, Augusto," Mary said.

Maxwell looked at Mary. "One bed or two?" he asked as he grabbed both of her hands and looked into her eyes, smiling.

"One. Definitely one," she said, rising to her tiptoes to kiss Maxwell. "It may be a very special night for you," she whispered in his ear.

"Oh?"

Augusto walked into the living room, holding a brochure. "Did you see all the things this ship has to do? It is incredible. You can surf, fly, climb a rock wall, swim ... They even have movies and a theatre. I wonder if the attractions have a weight limit."

"Did you know the food is free?" Maxwell asked. "All the food. Everything. Even the cheese!"

Mary smiled. "Yes."

"Is it possible to get closer to heaven on Earth?" Augusto asked. Just then, the ship's horn sounded, and he jumped.

"It's just the horn telling us we are departing," Mary explained.

"I am going to do some security reconnaissance and evaluate the food to make sure it is safe," Augusto said excitedly.

"Sure, go ahead," Mary said. She felt safe not that they had left the dock.

Maxwell and Mary went out onto the balcony to sit and enjoy the fresh air as they left Sydney Harbor.

"I am so happy we met, Maxwell. I need you." She placed her head on his shoulder. "These last few weeks have been crazy and terrifying. Can I ask you a serious question, though?"

"Anything."

"Are you rich? I mean, you seem to have a *lot* of money."

"Well, truthfully, I am. When I was sixteen, my dad invested money in Bitcoin for me in a custodial account when people did not understand it. It has paid off, and now I have millions. Do not worry, though; I will always be the flip-flop-wearing, untucked shirt, small-car-driving, houseplant-killing, clumsy guy you met in the coffee shop."

"How many millions?" Mary asked.

"Over half a billion."

"What? That is why you are always paying for everything. Are you trying to impress me? Because I am totally unimpressed."

"I had to see if you were a gold digger," he said jokingly. "But you are the most beautiful, gracious person I have ever met."

"Money has never been important to me," she said. "It is the worth of one's soul that matters." She heard herself say *one's soul*, but she had no idea where it had come from.

There was a knock on the door, and Mary went to answer it.

"Should you answer that?" Maxwell asked.

She paused. "Yes."

She opened the door, and three well-dressed men brought in buckets of wine and three charcuterie boards—one filled with olives from all over the world with little labels—a tray of fine chocolates and pastries, and a large basket of peach tea with three types of honey.

Mary looked at Maxwell as the men passed her to set the wine and food down. "A little excessive. How can we eat all this and go to dinner in a while?" she asked.

"What? This is a celebration, and I thought Augusto would be here. We have a refrigerator."

"If you need anything, Mr. Downs, just give us a ring," one of the men said.

"Absolutely. And thank you."

"I am going to take a bath before dinner," Mary said. "Did our stuff arrive?"

"I think so."

"Oh, I hope they did not bring Augusto's café burlap bag to the kitchen." She walked out to the area where they would have placed the bags, but Augusto's bag was not there. "Oh no. I had a feeling. Maxwell, can you call the concierge and ask them to locate the café burlap bag?"

"Sure." Maxwell immediately picked up the phone and asked for the concierge.

"Yes, Mr. Downs?"

"We are missing a burlap bag that says *café* on it. It is the luggage of someone in our party."

"Say again?" the concierge asked. "Did you say burlap bag luggage?"

"It's a long story. Can you locate it for me?"

"Yes, sir."

"And another thing, please bring up four white dresses—size eight—a white Michael Kors dinner purse, and a silver chain with a diamond cross pendant. The diamonds must be high quality. And, lastly, four black tuxedos—size thirty-four-inch waist, thirty-six-inch jacket—and eleven-and-a-half-size shoes to match. I am going to send a man named Augusto to also be fitted. He may need extra fabric. Bill everything to this cabin."

Maxwell hung up the phone and could hear Mary running the water into the large tub. "I had them place rose petals and rose milk bath in there for you," he said through the door.

"I see them. Thank you."

He imagined what her naked body looked like stepping into the rose bath and grew excited.

"Rose petals for a goddess," he said as he opened a bottle of wine. "I have a goddess for a girlfriend."

He poured a glass of wine, walked back out to the balcony, and sat down. Never in his wildest dreams would he have thought that he would be with Mary. He grew nervous thinking about what the night might bring and how to express his love to her.

He raised his arm and smelled his armpit. "Whew, I need a shower."

He took another sip of wine.

Chapter 30

GODDESS

Mary finished her bath, put on the plush robe and slippers provided, and then walked into the bedroom to finish getting ready for dinner. Laying on the bed were four white dresses, a jewelry box, four pairs of shoes, and a small white purse. She smiled because she had wondered what she could wear to dinner during the entire bath. She did not have much. Augusto had even less.

"Did you find my gifts, Mary?"

"Oh my, yes. Thank you so much. Did they find Augusto's bag?"

"Not yet, but I expect an update any minute," Maxwell told her. "How do you get a hold of him when you need him?"

"You really can't. He has no phone."

The phone rang.

"Mr. Downs," the concierge said, "we have located the burlap bag. It was in our coffee room."

"Fantastic." He hung up the phone. "Good news, Mary. They found it."

"Thank goodness. It's all he has."

"I am going to take a shower."

"Okay."

***

Maxwell was sitting on the couch, already showered and dressed, as he listened to Mary blow dry her hair. She then went back into the bedroom and emerged a few minutes later.

Maxwell was speechless as he watched her walk into the living room and stand in front of him in a long, white dress that followed the curves of her body to perfection. Her long, light brown hair fell over her shoulders in soft curls, and the diamond cross gleamed in the light.

"So," she asked, "how do I look?"

"You look like the most beautiful woman whom God has ever put on this planet—ever. A goddess of all goddesses."

"That will do," she said as she walked over to him and planted a kiss on his cheek.

Maxwell stood up. "Can I pour you a glass of wine?" he asked, walking over to the wine bucket.

"Sure. Has Augusto returned?"

"Not yet. I'm sure he is having the time of his life. I'm not as concerned about him on the ship as I would be if we were traveling by air, anyway. He has the skills to ward off threats."

Suddenly, Augusto burst through the door, all smiles. "Mary, you will not believe this ship! I already won two contests—one for the most *Avengers*-like and the tallest person. There is food everywhere, and I met some kids who asked for my autograph."

"Well, did you sign one for them?" she asked.

"Uh ... Yes. A little white lie. Then they started following me around, humming some song from *The Avengers*."

"We are going to dinner. Do you want to come or do your own thing?" Mary asked.

"Honestly, I just wiped out the sushi bar. The guy could not make them fast enough. I am stuffed. I will skip it. There is a movie I want to go check out ... unless you would like me to join you for security reasons."

"No," Mary said. "I think we will be okay. Do your thing."

"Stop in the men's shop to be fitted for clothes at some point," Maxwell told him. "I've already made the arrangements."

"Okay, but people are in awe to see a monk on a cruise," Augusto said. "I am really enjoying the attention."

***

On the way to the theater, a group of girls squeezed into the elevator with Augusto. One of them turned around and said, "Hi."

"Hi," he said back with an awkward wave.

She giggled while shyly covering her mouth with her hand.

Augusto thought she was beautiful, but he reeled in his emotions, remembering who he was—a monk from a French monastery.

The elevator doors opened, and before she stepped out, she turned back around and asked, "We are going to a movie. Would you like to join us?"

Augusto looked to either side of him, thinking she must be talking to someone else.

The doors started to close, and she inserted her foot to stop them. They opened again.

"Well, Mr. Monk, would you like to go with us to a movie?"

"Sure, I love movies," Augusto said.

As they walked together, she asked, "How did you land the role in *The Avengers*?"

He did not want to deflect her attention. Another harmless lie would not hurt.

"Well, I worked out a lot—I mean, *a lot*. I lifted very heavy blocks, and wheels of cheese, and barrels of coffee beans for months. Then I sent in a tape to my agent, who said they were looking for someone big and strong to play a monk. So, I got the role."

"You did? Cheese and coffee?" she asked sheepishly. "You are a real monk, aren't you?"

"Yes, I am a real monk," he said as they both laughed.

"What is your name?" the girl asked.

"Augusto. Yours?"

"Hana. It means *flower* in Japanese."

"Nice to meet you," Augusto said. "So, you are from Japan?"

"Yes."

"Me, too. My mother was from the Tohuko region, but she died when I was young."

"Do you speak Japanese?"

"Yes, French and English, also."

"*Anata wa kawairashī,*" Hana said in Japanese, testing him.

"Thank you," Augusto replied, blushing.

They arrived at the theater and sat down beside each other. Augusto barely fit in the seat.

"What is the movie?" he asked.

"It's the new *Avengers* movie."

"Seriously?" he asked as he settled in.

Chapter 31

DINNER

Mary and Maxwell arrived at the dining room and were escorted to a table. She was now the most beautiful woman in the room, and many wives were aware of this fact as their husbands' attentions focused directly on her as she gracefully walked by their tables. Some were so bold that they turned around to see her backside after she passed. She felt their gaze and silently whispered, "Sinners," to herself.

The men already seated at the table rose as Mary approached.

"Thank you, gentlemen," she said as the maître d' pulled out her chair for her.

The dinner conversation was cordial and straightforward. However, Mary yearned for a more in-depth talk about the events that occurred over the last few weeks. She needed to speak with Maxwell alone. She had so many questions.

The conversation continued at the table about nothing until one of the men at the table behind theirs started speaking about how political refugees from the Middle East should never be allowed into Christian countries. Maxwell could read the agitation growing on Mary's face.

This is the last thing she needs now, he thought.

After a few more minutes, Mary stood up and chastised the man. "Sir, we are all God's creations. Weren't you pushed out of your mother's vagina like every other person in this room and the world with absolute parental joy? A true gift from God?"

"Mary!" Maxwell exclaimed.

"What makes them different? Their skin color? Their beliefs? What makes you superior? Your skin color, money, and preaching of fear? Your mother must be so proud of your prejudice. These people are dying from influences beyond their control!"

The man sat there, red-faced, realizing his mistake as he looked around the room at the stares.

Mary grabbed her purse and walked away from the table and out of the dining room. The women in the room stood up and began clapping, and the men soon followed suit.

"I am so sorry," Maxwell said to the guests at their table, standing up and quickly following her.

"There was no need to apologize. That was epic!" one of the wives said.

The man who had commented stood up, apologized for his insolence, and then quickly left with his wife.

Maxwell caught up to Mary in the hall.

"I am sorry, Maxwell. I don't know what got into me. I just couldn't sit there without interjecting, listening to that man's poisoned perspective of humanity. The last thing this planet needs is more division. I don't know what I am saying. Is there another restaurant on the ship with a table that we can secure for just the two of us?"

"Yes, but please calm down. I want this night to be relaxing for you."

The maître d' walked up to where Mary and Maxwell stood. "Mr. Downs, I took the liberty of buying out the private chef's table for you and the beautiful lady, if you would like to take advantage of it?"

"Very good. We shall, and thank you."

"Follow me then." The maître d' started walking down the hall, toward the restaurant.

They arrived and were escorted to a long private table with its own staff, who were waiting.

"Perfect," Mary said as Maxwell pulled out the chair for her to sit.

Dinner was fantastic, and Mary felt at complete peace with Maxwell sitting across from her. She realized that her love for him was so strong that it would be difficult to explain to someone if asked. She did not want to speak about the dining room incident, and instead focused on their lives over the past few weeks and the sincerity and kindness of Augusto. She filled Maxwell in on how he had been banished to the lower cellar and wrote exceptional poetry as she tried to recite "Wild Dawn." She eventually gave up, laughing.

"I am so relieved to see you smiling after all you've been through," Maxwell told her.

"I know it's strange. It's as if I have a suit of emotional armor on. Don't get me wrong; the events that have occurred over the last few weeks have deeply affected me. But I feel like the scriptures of these events have already been written. Can you understand what I mean?"

"I think so. Just look at what you have accomplished."

The conversation turned more serious when Mary asked Maxwell, "Do you think I healed those people? At first, I tried to rationalize the events as coincidences, but truthfully, I am beginning to believe that there is some strange transition happening to me. I feel a new energy, and it is growing stronger, like in that church we visited in Newport. The words coming out of my mouth also seem different. I do not know what to think, but all I can say is that if I did heal Gustave and that baby, I am so grateful—confused, but grateful. I mean, it is impossible, right?"

"These days, I do not know if anything is impossible, Mary. I once knew a nurse who witnessed many miracles with little explanation. She would always say that this person was healed by the hand of God first and the science of medicine second."

"Well, you touch me, and nothing happens to you."

"I know it's weird, but maybe those you heal have some divine purpose. I have seen a subtle change in you, but I have not been with you long. All I know is that whatever is happening, it's all good."

"Yes, I guess so," Mary said.

"I wonder where Augusto is right now. He is probably driving the ship after he convinced the crew he was in *The Avengers*," Mary said, and they both broke out into laughter.

After dinner, they walked slowly back to the room, holding hands. Mary glanced at Maxwell, who stopped at a large window overlooking the sea and took in the moonlight and stars reflecting off the water.

"There is *Ursa Minor*, or little bear," he said, pointing toward the constellation.

"Oh, and there is *Orion*, the hunter, my favorite constellation," Mary said.

He turned to her and kissed her tenderly. She could feel him—his genuine love for her, his energy, his soul. She did not want the moment to end. These few seconds in time, everything was perfect.

Chapter 32

LOVE MAKE

"Let's go back to the room and have some peach tea," Mary said. "I had my eye on a large piece of chocolate from the charcuterie board."

"Absolutely," Maxwell said.

They walked back to the room. Surprisingly, Augusto was still out.

Maxwell poured bottles of spring water into a pot on the stove then began to heat it as Mary watched him from the couch with I-am-going-to-devour-you eyes.

"What kind of honey would you like?" he asked. "Let's see. We have some from Cape Cod, Australia, and Sweden. All made with different pollinators."

"I can wait for the tea or the chocolate," Mary said. She then stood up, walked over to the stove, grabbed Maxwell by the hand, and turned off the burner with the other. She led him into the bedroom.

"No tea then?" Maxwell asked.

"*Shh* ..." she hushed him as they entered the bedroom.

She pushed him onto the bed and laid on top of him, kissing him passionately. She stood up and unzipped her dress from behind, and it cascaded into a heap on the floor.

She stood there naked, and her body glistened in the reflective light of the sea shining through the window. She was flawless. He started fumbling with his tuxedo to shed it, but he fell off the bed.

"I'm all right," he said, jumping back up.

Mary giggled. "Let me help," she said as she walked over to him and began removing his tie, shirt, belt, and pants. Then

she pushed him back onto the bed and straddled him. Their energies, intertwined and surged into euphoria ecstasy.

***

Maxwell delicately tucked Mary's hair behind her ears then kissed her forehead.

"Wow …" she sighed out.

"Yes, wow," Maxwell repeated. He lay beside her, gently running his fingers up and down her body, marveling at its beauty as he traced every curve.

Eventually, Mary leaned over to Maxwell. "Let's do that again."

"I'm in."

They spent hours exploring each other's bodies with passion, to the point where they exhausted themselves in the early morning.

Chapter 33

BREAKFAST

"How did you sleep?" Augusto asked Mary and Maxwell when they both slowly walked out of the bedroom, a little sore.

Of course they hadn't slept, but Mary said they'd had a wonderful night, anyway. She was smiling as she and Maxwell sat down at the dining table and Augusto placed a hot cup of peach tea in front of them.

"I finished making your tea," he said. "Did you hear that loud banging all last night? I mean, how close is that dance club from here? What time do they close?"

"No, not at all," Mary said, knowing that she and Maxwell were the source.

"Anyway, I have a busy day. I am to meet Hana at the pool around one o'clock for games."

"Hana?" Mary asked.

"Oh, I did not see you to tell you. I made a new friend. She is from my home country of Japan. She is very nice, and we watched a movie together last night."

"Really?" Mary said. "Good for you."

"Oh, and I wrote a short story last night because I could not sleep with all the banging. You guys did not hear it?" He banged his fist on the table, demonstrating the sound. "First, it was slow, like bang ... bang ... bang. Then it got faster ... bang, bang, bang, bang, bang! Then some screaming silence. Then it would start all over again. I do not know what kind of dance that was. Anyway, do you want to hear the story?"

"Sure," Maxwell said. "Mary said you are an excellent writer. I would love to hear it."

"It is called 'Magneto,'" Augusto said. "Here it goes.

> *The magneto car hovered down the road and soon passed the line where the long shadows of buildings ceased, and the sunlight radiated uninterrupted from the heavens.*

"See, Mary? I used the word *heavens*."

"I see, Augusto."

> *The light danced on my sister's face, and she stirred.*

"I don't have a sister but always wanted one."

"OMG, Augusto, just keep reading. Don't stop," Mary urged.

> *The mood in the vehicle instantly changed as the Magneto passed by fields of green plants, trees, and penned animals.*
>
> *'This is so uplifting,' Hobart whispered to himself with his nose pressed against the glass to absorb every warm ray.*
>
> *There was a brightness to this area not found in New Urban, which was filled with stoic buildings that cast dark, muted shadows on the cold, hardened landscape below.*
>
> *'Where are we?' Hobart asked the driver, amazed at the new landscape he was seeing.*
>
> *'New Rural. It's a communal area that surrounds the urban centers. Only people with enough sun credits can access it,' the driver replied.*

The car sped past people working in the fields, and a small brown and white dog near the side of the road paused to watch them pass.

'Hey, sis, did you see that dog?'

She did not respond ... She was not looking around at all. Instead, her gaze was fixed on the seat in front of her.

My mom was on the New Urban Solar Rights Council and oversaw planning areas in chronic shade. My sister and I were now heading to Boston Urban to meet a doctor to diagnose her illness.

Boston was having recent riots about the lack of sunlight, but my mom weighed the risks and bought two tickets for passage; it was all she could afford. The rest, she must save for the special bulbs that we needed for the lightboxes. You could tell which houses could not afford them—the people living there were pale and sickly.

'How do they manipulate the light here?'

'Very large LM PRISMS in the upper atmosphere above the cloud that concentrates the sunrays enough to beam through the canopy. Two women invented them.'

'Wow. Why do they not do that in the urbans?'

'Politics and control,' the driver said.

New Urban used to be the great city of New York, but since the internet revolution, the names of all the cities had been changed to be descriptive with adjectives and even verbs. The change was necessary to meet the demands of a society that had no patience for words. People wanted concise sentences that described the noun—a person, place, or thing. Even my name, Hobart Health, was used to identify me as a person and our situation.

I was lucky. Many kids in my building on the lower floors had the adjective "sick" after their names. Little Margaret Sick was one of them, and the reason my mom was so passionate about sunlight rights.

SanFran Urban had been a great city once but had also dried up. No water and years of drought had caused great fires and an exodus to the mountains. It was a shame. Blatant overconsumption of resources mixed with pollution and climate change had ruined the entire city. We had known it was happening then—driving our cars here and there, throwing away plastics, consuming resources like ants.

We had gone through 'Save the Earth' movements over the last one hundred years to appease our consciousness. No significant sweeping actions were ever implemented worldwide.

Mom said human behavior was hard to change, that we were a species of convenience. Mom said it was like an old saying, 'peeing in the well.'

"I have more, but I have to go," Augusto said, shutting the notebook.

"Wait—what?" Mary exclaimed as she and Maxwell sat there dumbfounded. The story had been fantastic. "Are you sure you wrote that last night?" she asked, trying not to call him out directly.

"I sure did. Ever since you touched me, Mary, I have had these stories develop in my mind as I try to sleep. Words come to me like a never-ending fountain of literacy. See? There it is again. I don't outline or even think too much about where the story is going. I just write, pencil to paper. Did you like it?"

"There are no words on how good that story was. I am speechless at your talent," Mary said. "Maxwell, what did you think?"

"I agree with Mary—fantastic. Keep it up."

"I will. Thank you both. I am off to file a complaint about the banging. I need sleep."

Mary and Maxwell looked at each other.

"Good luck," Maxwell said.

"After that, I am off to the upper deck to check out the activities," Augusto said. "I have to meet my fan club. I will see you later then, good?"

"Fan club?" Mary asked then sighed. "Yes, all good."

Maxwell walked over to pick up the phone and order breakfast to be delivered to the room.

"We arrive in Tahiti today, right?" he asked as he hung up.

"I think so. I can't wait," Mary said, really enjoying the normalcy of this trip.

The phone rang, and Maxwell answered it. A woman on the other end said, "Mr. Downs, I am sorry to bother you, but we have received complaints about banging that may be coming from your room. It is disturbing some of our guests."

"Yes, ma'am, I see. I believe it is one of my guests. He brought three women here last night and told me he likes tying them up to the headboard while having wild sex."

Mary was aghast then laughed into her hands, trying not to spoil the fun.

The woman was silent on the other end of the phone, probably not knowing what to say.

"I think she dropped the phone," he said, turning to Mary.

Finally, the woman responded, "*The Avengers?*"

"Yes, ma'am, *The Avengers*," Maxwell said. "I will talk to him today and ask him to reduce the number of women he will bring back tonight to two and tie them to the couch, or dining room table, or something."

"Uh ... Let me see ... I should get someone else to speak to him."

"No need, ma'am. I will speak to him."

Maxwell hung up the phone, and he and Mary burst into laughter.

Mary fell on the floor, laughing uncontrollably. Then she composed herself and said, "I am going to take a shower."

Maxwell heard the water running and decided to step into the shower with her.

She hugged him as the water fell upon them both. He could see her better now, and she was more beautiful in the light. He began kissing her neck, which soon turned into him ravishing her again. He could not get enough of her, and she of him. The feeling was magical.

Mary kissed him passionately then said, "I need to take a shower so we can enjoy this ship. We will pick this up again tonight. You're a machine."

"Okay. I love you," he said as he stepped out of the shower to dry off.

"I love you, too."

In the shower, Mary thought about the fantastic sex that she and Maxwell had had the night before and that, even if she was someone special or becoming someone special, she was also human. Consensual sex between two lovers was not a sin. Never a sin.

Chapter 34

TAHITI

Mary, Maxwell, and Augusto walked down the gangplank and passed the native greeters to catch an awaiting boat, which Maxwell had the concierge arrange for the trip to the island of Morea.

Mary wanted to skip the urbanized area and experience the beauty of French Polynesia. She wanted to focus on finding the places that they had seen in photos, with crystal clear waters and white-sand beaches fringed with coconut palm trees swaying in the warm breeze, and she also wanted privacy.

"It's strange," Augusto said as he walked behind Mary and Maxwell toward the dock. "All of the women who work on the ship now want to talk to me. A few told me when they get off work, and some even asked me to dinner."

"Really? That is strange. Do they know you are a real monk?" Mary asked.

"Uh … Maybe not. About that … I have decided to leave the monastery, renounce my vows, and return to Japan once you are safe."

"Really, Augusto?" Mary asked. She stopped walking to turn and look at him.

"Yes, I have made up my mind. I will not return to the monastery's lower cellar in France. I have a new mission—to write—and I am interested in Hana. We have something. Besides, I think I have broken so many vows on this trip that I will have to confess for decades. I spoke to Hana about meeting her sometime in the future and trying to join another monastery in Japan, if the opportunity arises. I am still a child of God."

"I think that is best for you, knowing how you were treated. It was abuse, Augusto," Mary said. "Let's talk about it more later, okay?"

They found the boat and boarded.

"Captain, how long is the trip to Morea?" Mary asked.

"About half an hour. Please, take a seat. I am not the regular captain of this boat. My friend asked me to fill in for him. My name is Claude. I am French," he said as he winked at Mary. Claude had a medium build; dark, oily hair; bad teeth; and a creepy air about him.

She ignored him.

The captain cast off the lines and powered up the engine to pull away from the dock.

Suddenly, a woman in a royal blue cloak ran down the dock, jumped over the water, and into the boat. Augusto, who had been sitting, immediately stood up, taking a defensive position.

"Who are you?" he asked. "How did you find us?"

"I have been assigned to Mary and Maxwell by the Collective," she said.

"Words?" Augusto asked her, to Mary's surprise.

"*Solomon, Sancti Martini, Cathedralis Trevirensis, Magddo Church.*"

"You are from the European Collective, then?" he asked.

"Yes. My name is Thea."

"She seems legitimate," Augusto told Mary and Maxwell. "It's your call. Should she stay or go?"

"If I go, I am bound by oath to follow you," Thea said.

Maxwell looked at Mary. "She can stay, but please do not interfere with our enjoyment and do not impose on us."

"Understood. You will not know I am here."

The captain powered up the boat again, and they headed off to Morea. Thea stood next to the captain, looking ahead.

"You look hot in that cloak. You may want to take it off at some point and show me how fit you are. I am French," the captain said with a wink then stuck out his tongue.

She reached over, grabbed his balls, and squeezed hard. The boat veered to the right.

"I am only kidding, *mademoiselle*," he said. "Kidding. Calm down."

Thea walked away from him and sat near the stern.

***

Augusto stared at Thea for some time before he decided to grab a soda from the cooler marked "*Drinks*" to her right. He carefully approached and noticed the *C* pin on her cloak.

"I always wanted one of those," he said as he reached into the cooler, grabbed a soda, and stood up. "May I see it?"

"Sure," Thea said.

Augusto pushed Thea off the gunwale with great strength, sending her into the water as the boat kept speeding along.

Everyone looked to the rear of the boat, hearing the loud splash.

"Man overboard! Woman overboard!" the captain shouted as he powered down the engine and began to turn around.

"Leave her," Augusto ordered as he walked up to him.

"What?" the captain exclaimed.

"Leave her. She is not who she says she is. She is a threat."

"What are you doing? How is she a threat?" Mary yelled over the engine noise.

Maxwell had grabbed the life ring and was about to throw it.

"Everyone stop!" Augusto boomed.

"We must retrieve her, Augusto," Mary said as she watched Thea drift farther and farther from the boat.

"No," Augusto replied.

"Augusto you are a man of God," Mary's voice grew louder and more desperate.

Augusto looked at Mary, then Maxwell, who nodded in agreement.

"Captain let's pick her up," he said and the engines powered back up.

Thea was wide-eyed, treading water as the boat pulled close to her.

"Not too close, Captain," Augusto instructed.

"If we do not get her out of the ocean soon, the reef sharks will find her," the captain said, concerned.

"Your pin," Augusto yelled to her, "it's not authentic! It's a fake, and you are probably, too. Who are you really?"

She didn't answer as a large shadow passed under the boat, under her.

Thea seemed to notice it, also, as she looked down in the water. Her face was now full of fear.

"Who are you?" Augusto demanded.

Another large, dark shadow swam by her. There were now two.

"Pretty soon, there will be fifty sharks circling her," the captain said. "We have to pull her into the boat. I do not want a death on my record. It will ruin me."

Augusto was torn. He wanted to leave her there to suffer her fate—that was his training—but he was a child of God and did not have it in him.

"Shed all your clothes, place them in your right hand, and then we will throw you the life ring and pull you back on board."

"I will not," Thea responded, growing upset.

"Augusto, is this necessary?" Mary asked, standing next to him. "Her dignity."

"She is probably a trained killer, sent by them to harm you. Or worse. We cannot risk it."

He turned to Thea. "It's your choice."

The number of sharks seemed to increase with every second. Thea was crying now as she pulled off her royal blue cloak and the rest of her clothes. She was now completely nude, swimming among the sharks.

"Throw her the ring," Augusto instructed Maxwell. This was not something Augusto wanted to do, but it had to be done this way.

Maxwell threw her the ring, and she caught it.

"Slowly now, *mademoiselle.* Do not make any sudden moves or splashes," the captain said as Maxwell pulled her in. "You sure are fit," the captain then said as he watched Thea approach the boat.

Mary angrily glanced at him.

When she was within a foot, Augusto heaved her in with one arm, grabbing her clothes with the other. "Stand near the stern," he instructed.

Slowly, Thea walked to the stern, defeated, naked, and vulnerable.

"Augusto, I ask again," Mary said, "is this necessary?"

"Who are you?" he asked Thea, ignoring Mary.

Thea was crying as she looked up to see eight eyes staring at her nakedness. She looked down in embarrassment.

"I was sent from the Third Order to report Mary's position to the First Order," she finally said. "I am just a messenger, not a killer. I was demoted to the position because I could not harm anyone."

"What is your name? It really is Thea?" Mary asked, her compassion for the woman growing.

"Augusto, I have had enough. Give her something to cover herself with."

She then turned toward Maxwell. "Please bring me some towels from below deck."

Mary took the towels from Maxwell when he returned and handed them to Augusto, who threw them at Thea.

"Cover yourself, and then I will tie your hands for safety and place you below deck."

Thea covered herself as best she could, and then Augusto tied her hands and secured her to a wooden post below deck.

"What are we going to do with her?" Mary asked.

"Not much. We will leave her with the captain while we continue on with our day," Augusto said. "Once we are back on the big island, I will let her go. She is a Third Order, the lowest rank in the organization."

"What organization?" Mary asked.

"The one after you."

"I don't feel it. I don't feel as if she has an evil soul." She stepped on her tiptoes, trying to get close to Augusto's ear. "I do not like the idea at all, of leaving her with the captain. He seems like a slimebag."

"It's the only choice."

When they arrived at the Morea dock, Maxwell noticed a waiting car, arranged by the concierge.

Mary walked over to the captain, looked him straight in the eyes, and said, "If you hurt that woman, the wrath of God will descend upon you." Then she brushed his hand with hers.

"I wouldn't dare," he said in a serious tone.

At the car, the driver introduced himself. "Hi, Mr. Downs, I am your driver, Rai." The man grabbed each of their backpacks and placed them in the trunk. "I hear you are looking for a private place to relax. So, my cousin owns a villa on the island, on the water, with a pool, hammocks, and a small white-sand beach. She lets me use it when she is away on business. It is a little paradise for only two hundred fifty US dollars a day and comes with my other cousin, Talei. She will serve you drinks and make authentic Fijian food."

"Great. Sounds perfect," Maxwell said.

Rai dialed his phone. "Talei, we have guests today who would like to experience Fijian hospitality. I should be arriving in twenty-five minutes." He hung up.

They traveled down the main road, stopping at little boutiques to buy souvenirs and bathing suits for the long day at the pool and beach. So far, no one seemed to have recognized Mary.

Rai spent most of the drive talking about the island's interesting facts and must-see attractions, often letting go of the wheel as he talked with his hands.

"I recommend a restaurant called K on the island, if you are still here for dinner," Rai said as he pulled up to the villa driveway. "Here is my number. Call when you are ready for me to deliver food, lunch, or to depart. Anything you need, I can deliver to you, Mr. Downs."

"Fantastic," Maxwell said, handing him a fifty US dollar.

As they approached the front door of the villa, a beautiful Fijian woman, with perfect bronze skin and long black hair, opened it. She wore a brightly colored floral wrap.

"*Bula*," she said as they entered, handing each of them a drink with a tiny, colorful umbrella impaling pieces of pineapple, banana, and papaya.

"I need the strongest drink possible," Mary said as she took one. She noticed a table full of fresh-cut fruit and flowers laid out on a large banana leaf.

"Make yourself at home," the woman said. "The villa is yours."

They walked into the living room, seeing the entire back wall was glass that opened onto a pool deck, and then a white-sand beach with coconut palms and two hammocks. Crystal-clear blue waters framed the setting. The view was just what Mary had hoped for.

"Oh, Maxwell, this place is amazing," she said as she gave him a big hug and kiss.

Chapter 35

SACRIFICE

As soon as the car was out of sight, the captain gleefully ran to the market and picked up a case of beer, almost skipping back to the boat. Once onboard, he cast off the lines and left the dock, heading out to sea.

Thea grew nervous when she heard the engines start again.

After about half an hour, he walked down to where she was tied up and slapped her hard across the face, again and again. "Now we are going to see how fit you are," he said.

***

Mary was lying on the beach with a drink in hand, thinking about Thea and how she could have ended up on the side of evil. Had she been recruited or forced into the Third Order? She seemed so young. Only in her early twenties. Her soul was misguided.

Mary decided to walk out into the water to take a dip, look for shells, and cool off. As she stepped into the water and began walking along the beach, she noticed a school of interesting fish nearby. The largest was about thirteen inches with a long, needle-like snout. She would walk, and they would follow.

They are so cute. I wonder if they are waiting for food, she thought.

She yelled to Maxwell, who was lying in a lounge chair, "You should see these fish. They are adorable and bizarre."

He was sleeping and did not answer.

"I must have worn him out last night," she said to herself.

She dipped her body in the warm ocean waters again and relaxed. The fish were gone.

Talei was waiting on the beach with a towel and drink, handing them to Mary as she sat back down in the lounge chair.

"This is a slice of heaven," Mary said as she lay back to soak up more sun. "Talei, have you ever seen a long, thin, silvery fish with a very long mouth around here? Are they native to these waters? There were about nine of them following me up and down the shore."

"Yes, *mademoiselle*, that is the needlefish, or *sa'u*. They are common in these waters. They can swim and jump over fifty-six kilometers per hour."

"Interesting," Mary said as she opened her book and began to read.

***

The captain stood in front of Thea as she squirmed to free herself. She could see the shade of his body through her closed eyelids as he moved closer and closer.

"Please, señor, don't," she pleaded as she felt him place his hand on her thigh. She started praying in Spanish.

In an instant, the shade disappeared, and she heard a *thud*. She opened her eyes and looked at the deck, where he had been standing. He was there, crumpled, with a seven-inch, needle-like fish sticking entirely through his neck. There were several other fish also flapping around on the deck. The fish had severed his jugular, and he was quickly bleeding out and convulsing. She turned away.

"What the hell?" she exclaimed, trying to break free, squirming. She did not want to be near his evil soul, even in death. However, she could not free herself and continued to cry as she watched his blood slowly claim the areas around his body.

***

The group returned to the dock and noticed that their boat wasn't there. Maxwell asked a few locals, and they said it had left soon after it had arrived. A little panicked that they would not make it back to the ship in time, Maxwell saw another boat getting ready to leave that had just dropped off tourists. He ran to speak to the captain then motioned to Mary and Augusto to board. Once everyone was on board, they headed back into the ocean to go back to the ship.

"I am going to find Captain Claude and give him a piece of my mind," Maxwell told Mary.

As they neared the halfway point between the islands, Mary spotted an anchored boat not too far from them.

"Hey, isn't that the boat we took over?" she asked.

"It looks like it," Maxwell said. "Where is everyone? It looks empty. Hey, Captain, another fifty dollars if you can pass close to that boat anchored over there."

"Absolutely," the captain said as he turned toward it.

As they drew close, Maxwell could not believe what he saw.

Thea was lying naked on the deck, tied up and covered in blood, and the captain lay dead at her feet with a fish through his neck.

Mary gasped then noticed Maxwell leaning over the other side of the boat.

"I feel sick," he said.

Thea looked up at Augusto and Mary. "Please, help me." Severe sunburn covered her body in areas where the blood had not caked dry on her skin.

"Augusto, untie her, gently wash the blood off her, and then let's get out of here," Mary said.

The mortified captain ran below deck to grab a first-aid kit and a blanket.

Mary knew he was a good witness to the situation and valuable to Thea.

Augusto carried Thea on deck as Mary wrapped her in the blanket. He gently placed her down on a bench where the captain laid down towels to make it softer. She was obviously in shock.

Mary sat down next to Thea and stared at her hands in disbelief. "Did he violate you?" she whispered.

"No," Thea responded. "The fish killed him before he could."

Relieved, Mary knew that *she* had somehow saved Thea from this man and that it was the wrath of God who had delivered a swift judgment.

"I feel so guilty ... leaving her with that man. I should have listened to your judgment," Augusto said solemnly.

Mary reached out to him. "It was a mistake. I should have made my concerns stronger. We all make mistakes."

Chapter 36

THIRD ORDER

The boat's radio erupted in chatter after the captain had called in the crime to the authorities.

"I have an ambulance waiting at the dock, but the authorities will want a statement from everyone first," the captain told Maxwell.

They pulled up to the dock as two police boats sped past them, heading out into the open ocean.

Once the boat was tied up, another police officer met them and walked them to the waiting ambulance, asking what had happened. Surprisingly, Thea did not implicate Augusto, Mary, or Maxwell. Instead, she portrayed them as her saviors from the situation, saying that, without them, she would have been killed. The officers were interested in how the fish had killed the captain, but she could not tell them since Thea's eyes had been closed.

"I know about the dangers of needlefish and their ability to take flight and impale people. Many people have been severely injured, and some have died. It happens more frequently than people realize," the officer said. "But, usually, not during the daytime. That is odd."

The police officer took everyone's statement then released Augusto, Mary, and Maxwell to return to the ship. Mary was surprised that Thea didn't file any charges against them for how she had been treated.

Thea was sitting in the ambulance, crying and shaking, as Mary approached her.

"How are you feeling?"

"I'm okay," Thea said. "But it's going to take time."

"I would like you to meet us in Hawaii when the ship docks. Then I want to take you to the States. I do not feel you are an evil person."

"Maybe, but I have no money. The Third Order keeps everyone destitute, so we are dependent upon them for everything."

"You must leave the Third Order immediately, Thea."

"I have been trying to for several years and want to return to my home country of Columbia, to be with my family, but I cannot with no money."

"I will be right back," Mary said. She quickly walked over to where Maxwell and Augusto stood. She overheard them talking about the needlefish that had killed the captain.

"Excuse me, Maxwell. Would you help Thea return to her home in Columbia? I want her to join us after that in New York. I feel that she is not a threat, just trapped in a bad situation."

"Absolutely. What does she need?"

"Money."

"Are you sure you want to give it to her?" he asked.

"Yes, I forgive her. I have a feeling that she is not a bad person."

"Okay, how much?"

"I would suspect a couple thousand dollars."

"Done," Maxwell said.

Mary gave him a big hug and kiss.

"I see an ATM over there by the reception area," Maxwell said. "I will be right back."

Maxwell withdrew the money and walked back to Mary, handing it to her. She grabbed Thea's hand and placed the money in it.

Thea instantly felt some sort of energy pass through her hand, up her arm, and into her entire being.

"Please, forgive us, Thea," Mary said. "We should not have left you with that man."

Thea nodded silently. "And please, forgive me for my intentions," she said, looking up at her with tears in her eyes. Images of her speaking to large crowds in front of a large cross in Columbia suddenly flashed in her head. She did not know what to make of them.

"Bye for now," Mary said, having a feeling that they were destined to meet again.

Mary, Maxwell, and Augusto walked back to the ship and went up to their room.

***

"What a wonderful and terrible day combined. It's hard to explain. We need to decompress." Mary sat on the couch in the suite, reading *My Inventions: The Autobiography of Nikola Tesla* as the ship drew nearer to Hawaii. "Did you know that Nikola Tesla suffered from white flashes that interrupted his vision during most of his childhood? He also had many quirks and aversions to certain things and the ability to envision geometry and mathematics so that he did not need to draw up plans before he built his inventions. Thinking of his achievements, that is absolutely fascinating."

"I did not know that," Maxwell said.

"Yes, I am reading his autobiography now, trying to figure out what may be happening to me, with the new energy I am feeling."

"Why him?"

"Because he was a genius who focused on energy. He contributed so much to technology. He seemingly was not from this world. Anyway, can we talk about the tower now that Augusto has gone to lunch? I have written down the finds that we have made so far. Can I read them to you?"

"Sure."

"Okay, this is what I found. The cat is a symbol that is associated with the Knights Templar. I find it odd that it is on the tower. When the Knights Templar were being hunted and tortured in the early 1300s by the French king, 'worshipping a cat' was one of the charges of heresy.

"The lion in Christianity represents Jesus. I think this is a solid lead, referenced in the scriptures. It seems that the cat's position just above the lion has some sort of significance. The knight looks to be a Templar. I see a cross on his chest, which was a signature of their tunic. The face of the creature he is holding is still a mystery. It is pig-like, but I am still searching other ancient structures in Europe and the Middle East to see if there is a match.

"Remember that the knight was facing left? What if the direction has meaning? Could he be looking at some sort of writing or symbol?"

"Let me grab my phone, and I will pull the photo up," Maxwell said.

Maxwell returned from the bedroom with his phone and sat next to Mary on the couch. The photo loaded, and they both looked at it intensely, focusing on the direction of the knight's face.

"You know, it does seem that there is something there," Mary said. "He is facing left, and the stones are straight in a line. I wonder if the stucco-type material obscured what he is looking at."

"It's not clear. I also see the cross on his chest. This is great progress, Mary. I am excited about my thesis."

Chapter 37

RISE

Maxwell turned on the TV. After a few minutes, a photo of Mary popped up on the screen with a story about a woman who could heal people. A reporter was interviewing a couple standing in front of a crowd in Sydney, holding crosses and signs that read, "*A NEW HOPE FOR HUMANITY*" and "*HOPE FOR HUMANITY*," but the *H*, *M*, and *A* were crossed out, spelling "*UNITY*."

"Uh ... Mary, you should see this."

Mary walked into the living room from the kitchen and looked at the screen. "Oh no!" she exclaimed as she sat down on the couch.

"Hey, that is John and Elizabeth, the two people we met in Melbourne. Remember them?"

"Yes, but what are they doing?"

The reporter placed her microphone near a podium to listen in.

"*What do you see in the word* humanity? *What does it mean to you? We see* human, man, *and* unity. *If just twenty of you in this crowd spread the new message of unity and hope through your communities and on social media to people who you can touch, no matter what you believe in, no matter who you are or* where you are from, this is what the world needs right now. We challenge everyone in this crowd to extend empathy, friendship, love, hope, or whatever you would like to call it in your world. Let's send a message to the warmongers to realize what they are fighting for, or against, is not politics, land, and resources. It is ego, fire, and dust. What would the world be like without warmongers?" John said.

Someone in the crowd yelled, "*Better off!*"

"*Look around you. Are we so different? DNA testing of the world's population has shown the skeptics that we are all related somehow or another. It is undeniable. Are we enslaving, suppressing, fighting, injuring, and killing our brothers and sisters? Are we?*"

The woman grabbed the microphone and continued, "*The warmongers think they will be victorious and survive with their war machines … Let me tell you, they will not! A message has been sent from the heavens that someone is here on this continent as we speak, and her name is* Mary!"

The crowd cheered.

The reporter came back on screen. "*This movement is now spreading through Europe and here in Australia and Japan. There seems to be something happening, a new energy, a new hope galvanized around a woman named Mary. This is Isabelle Adamni for ABC.*"

"Oh my God!" Mary cried out. "What is happening? How are we going to continue with this? I did not ask for this."

Maxwell sat next to Mary on the couch. "Think about it. It is all good. Apparently, you are well protected by the Collective. Remember what Dr. Strum said to us in the park? I now believe something—and I cannot believe I am saying this—and that is that *you* are meant for a greater purpose. You are, as they say, Mary of Bethlehem, the one who can see. I wonder what else you can do." He winked at her.

"Maxwell, this is serious. How can we even enjoy the last days on this ship with all the photos, posts, and exposure? We are going to be at risk."

Maxwell thought about it. She had a point.

He picked up the phone to call the concierge. "I will rent a private jet to bring us back to Long Island's MacArthur Airport ... after we spend some time in Hawaii. How about we find an Airbnb that is secluded?"

"Sounds great."

Over the next few days, they tried to enjoy all the ship had to offer. Many people came up to Mary to see her, almost as if she were a curiosity. Augusto and the ship's security were always by her side and would not let anyone near or touch her. Photos being snapped of her were uncontrollable and seemed almost constant wherever she went. She would not look at social media because she knew her acts were going viral worldwide, deeply worrying her.

Chapter 38

HAWAII

As the ship docked at the Hawaiian port, Mary, Maxwell, and Augusto gathered their things, preparing to disembark. Augusto knew getting Mary off the ship and into a car would be a challenge. She had achieved a sort of weird celebrity status.

Just as they were prepared to leave, there was a knock at the door.

"I'll answer it." Maxwell walked over to the door and opened it.

Standing there was Mary's dad and four bores.

"Can I help you? Are you the ship's security detail?" Maxwell asked the men, not recognizing them.

"No, Maxwell, I am Mary's dad. May we come in?"

Shocked, Maxwell muttered, "Yes, I guess so."

"Who is it?" Mary asked from the bedroom.

"Uh ... Mary, it's a guy who says he is your dad with four huge men."

"Damn," Mary whispered to herself, having known it would just be a matter of time before he had found her again.

She decided to embrace his arrival, realizing that things had really accelerated with social media.

"Dad, I am so glad you found us," Mary said, half-lying as she walked over and hugged him.

He did not look happy, and the bores even less so.

"You are coming with us," her father said, grabbing her by the elbow to lead her out of the room. Instead, she jerked her arm out of his grip and faced him.

"I am going nowhere without Augusto and Maxwell," she said, raising her voice.

The bores now surrounded Augusto and Maxwell.

Augusto turned to Maxwell. "I am growing really angry witnessing this situation, but it is her dad. What can we do?"

"They are at risk, too!" Mary yelled as she ran to the bathroom and locked the door.

Her dad ran after her. "Mary, open the door now. We must leave."

"No, not until you reassure me that Augusto and Maxwell are coming with us."

"They cannot."

"Dad, they saved me from many harmful situations, and Augusto knows things that your security does not. I am not leaving without them."

Her dad pulled out a cell phone and made a quick call. "Okay, they will come with us," he said after hanging up. "We must move. The crowd on the wharf is growing enormous."

The bores grabbed the luggage, and they headed to the gangplank. Mary and Maxwell were shocked to see the size of the crowd waiting on the wharf.

"Let's go," Mary's dad said.

They ran down the gangplank and tried to get through the crowd to two parked SUVs. However, the crowd surged forward, and the first barricades fell. Mary and Maxwell were pinned against a fence with her dad and the bores in front, trying to push the crowd back. It was not working.

"They are hurting me. I am being crushed!" Mary yelled.

The ship's captain saw what was happening and sounded the horn to startle people. He then came over to the loudspeaker.

"Ladies and gentlemen, people are getting hurt. This is an unsafe situation. Please, leave the wharf area immediately."

The crowd was now in a frenzy trying to see Mary, touch her.

"Dad, help me!"

"Fire," her dad said to the bores.

Two bores pulled out their handguns, and each fired a shot in the air. Mary knew this would go badly, but it was their last resort.

The crowd panicked. People started running and screaming in all directions. Many fell and were trampled.

"Now is our chance," her dad said as he grabbed Mary's hand.

They ran a few yards, and Mary saw a young father kneeling next to a young girl, yelling for help.

"She's not breathing, she's not breathing, she's not breathing!" he screamed, but no one stopped.

Mary pulled out of her dad's grip and ran over to the little girl. She must have been no more than six years old.

"Mary, no!" her dad yelled.

"Thank you," the little girl's father said. "Are you a doctor?"

"No."

Mary did not wait for the father to say anything else. She grabbed the little girl and leaned her up, saying a prayer close to her ear as she placed her hand on her forehead. This time, she felt the energy pass through her, out of her hand, and into the little girl's body. The little girl drew a deep breath and started crying. Confused, she looked around until she saw her dad.

"Daddy, I went up into the sky, but they said I had to come back," she said.

"What?" her dad said, now kneeling next to her, hugging her in disbelief.

"You should leave," Mary said to the father as she stood up. She looked around and saw other people lying on the ground. *Oh God, please help them.*

Paramedics were now arriving on the scene, running toward the injured.

Thorsen grabbed her hand more firmly now and began to run to the SUVs.

Augusto and Maxwell were already sitting in one of the SUVs, watching Mary and her dad run toward them. Before they could get close, however, a man in a black cloak emerged from the dispersing crowd and started toward Mary.

"Mary, a First Order, a First Order!" Augusto yelled from the car, watching the situation unfold before him as he tried to undo his seat belt.

"Shoot that guy!" Augusto ordered the bores, but they could not with the crowd.

Once the man was near Mary, he took out a large wooden staff with a knotty bulb on the end from under his cloak and swung it hard. Her dad tried to intercept the blow, but it glanced off his arm as the man kicked him to the side, and it landed hard on Mary's skull. She fell to the ground.

"*No!*" Augusto cried out. He and Maxwell were now out of the SUV, running toward the man, with the bores in tow.

Mary was still lying on the ground, semiconscious, rolling back and forth and moaning in pain when Maxwell knelt by her side. He picked her up and started running toward the SUV with her dad. The SUV was now driving toward them.

Augusto never slowed down, and as he drew near the man, he punched him in the face, and the man careened backward to the ground. Augusto brought his knee down hard on the man's ribcage, which was met with a concert of cracking bone. He then took his arms and broke them both, holding one end for leverage and bringing down his massive foot as you would on a piece of firewood. Two bores stood there, watching with surprise.

"I would kill you, but I am a man of God," he said with rage as he slowly stood up.

The man smiled with blood-drenched teeth. "You are on the wrong side of this war."

Augusto looked around and saw that the paramedics and the remaining crowd close by were staring at him as if he were a monster.

"Augusto, get in," Maxwell said as the SUV pulled up to where he stood.

Augusto and the bores quickly hopped into the SUV and drove off.

Trying to calm down, Augusto turned around to see the aftermath of the fight. The paramedics were now by the man's side, working on his injuries. He felt bad for him, knowing he was just following a directive from the oracle—the supreme commander of The Order.

He questioned his rage, the intensity of it, the origin, the hatred—all of it, all the emotion that fueled it. The more he thought about it, the more it was pointing toward his father, how he had been treated at the abbey, and what he had been taught, whether it was right or wrong—acceptance but division. He wondered how a pacifist, whose purpose was to worship God, became weaponized to invoke pain on another human being.

He looked at Mary lying across the seat, and his guilt faded into anger. She was badly injured. He loved her, and to protect her was his divine purpose.

Chapter 39

SOLOMON PROTOCOL

Thorsen and Maxwell were in the back seat of the SUV with Mary lying across their laps. Augusto and a bore were stuffed into the third seat. No one said a word.

Thorsen picked up his cell phone with the uninjured arm and slowly dialed with one hand. Maxwell heard someone pick up the other end.

"Mary has been injured. Therefore, I invoke the Solomon Protocol. Have the plane ready at the Daniel K. Inouye International Airport with a medical team. We will be there in twenty-five." He looked at his watch then clicked off the call.

"Where the fuck were you guys?" Thorsen said angrily to the bores. "This should have never happened. This cannot happen. She is my daughter!"

"Sir, we went ahead to secure a path to the vehicles when she broke away to attend to that little girl."

"No, you ass, you are *never* to leave her ... *ever*. Do you understand? You *always* stay with her. I do not care what she does. You stay with her."

Mary was going in and out of consciousness, moaning.

"Driver faster," Thorsen said, and the driver sped up.

"Where was the Collective?" Maxwell asked.

"I do not know. Maybe they were not activated here yet. But, if they were, my guess is that they took them out before the attack. We should hear more about it on the news. Maybe some of the other people lying on the ground were from the Collective. This organization is well trained. They would have used the panic of the crowd as cover."

The car sped into the airport, where the private planes were kept. A jet was warming its engines, preparing for takeoff. They pulled up, and several people with a stretcher ran toward them. They carefully pulled Mary out of the SUV, laid her on the stretcher, and then carried her into the waiting jet.

"Come on, guys; let's board," Thorsen said to everyone standing around, looking concerned. "She is in good hands."

They all boarded and sat in seats indicated by a flight attendant. The plane started to taxi and soon took off.

"Where are we heading, Mr. ... I'm sorry. What is your name?" Maxwell asked.

"My name is Mr. Bill. We are heading to where the First Temple in Jerusalem was constructed—Temple Mount. Today, we know it as the Dome of the Rock."

"Okay, Mr. Bill." Maxwell knew he did not have much say in the situation, but it was good to know.

He looked around and was impressed with the plane's interior. There was a nice kitchen and bar, a large computer area, a few sleeping compartment with beds and plush chairs on either side, and toward the rear was a partitioned-off medical room. He could see the doctors working on Mary through the glass.

After an hour, the doctor came out.

"Mr. Bill, she is going to be okay. There is no bleeding on the brain, and her skull is intact. It's just time to heal and rest, and she will be fine."

"I guess the deflection of the staff off my arm saved her," Thorsen said.

"Yes, I think it did."

"Can we see her?" Maxwell asked.

"Not yet," the doctor said. "Please, give her some time to heal."

"Settle in, guys," Thorsen said. "This is going to be a long flight."

"How long?" Maxwell asked.

"Seventeen hours."

"Oh boy," Maxwell replied. "Luckily, I have my phone."

"No, sir, I need all of your cell phones and computers, if you have one," Thorsen said. "We are now in Solomon Protocol—off the grid."

A bore got up and collected all the cell phones, handing them to another bore now sitting at the computer station.

"Don't worry," Thorsen said. "He will not access them. We have a lot of damage control to do now that the world is aware of Mary. I was hoping it would not have gone this way, but she is a woman of strong will."

"Mr. Bill, can I ask you why the man attacked her with a wooden staff? Seems odd," Maxwell said. "Why didn't anyone shoot him?"

"I asked the bores to shoot him," Augusto interjected.

"There were too many people," Thorsen said. "My understanding is that the First Order only uses weaponry from the ancient times—the bow, arrow, Atal, spear, and staff. One should never underestimate them, though. The staff he used was as hard as steel. It almost broke my arm." He pulled up his sleeve to show a sizeable purpling bump where the staff had hit him.

A call on his cell phone interrupted him. He answered but did not speak.

"Your monk almost killed my son. He will not recover fully, Thorsen. We are raising the effort to eliminate Mary so the holy genetic line will end with her."

"I do not control the monk," Thorsen said angrily then hung up.

"Who was that?" Maxwell asked.

"Once a member of my family, but now an enemy," Thorsen answered.

Chapter 40

JERUSALEM

The plane arrived in Jerusalem, and they waited for the stretcher that Mary was laying on to be loaded into an ambulance before settling in the two waiting SUVs.

"Temple Mount seems like a strange place to take us, Mr. Bill," Maxwell said.

"I understand, but these events, that you are now a part of, were set in motion thousands of years ago."

"Augusto, you sure are quiet," Thorsen commented.

"I failed, sir. I failed to protect her."

"Do not be so hard on yourself. Mary has a very strong will, and she does what she wants. Remember how she broke away from us all to tend to that child? Besides, she will be fine."

"Maybe. I just wish she would have regained consciousness already," Augusto reclined back in his seat.

The SUV continued to speed along the narrow streets of Jerusalem, past the whitewashed buildings and bustling vendors, toward Temple Mount. Maxwell was silent, looking out the window, not wanting to look at Mary. After twenty minutes he spoke.

"Where are we going?" Maxwell asked when they stopped and got out of the SUV, heading toward a tunnel.

The walls around them were made of massive stone blocks decorated with what looked to be ancient murals of Knights Templar battles and holy scenes. Now and then, they passed a wooden door, and as they walked, cameras seemed to follow them as they passed through several ancient iron gates. At the end of the tunnel, they reached a door that led into a room with high vaulted ceilings and modern amenities. There were computers, huge televisions, nice furniture, and a kitchen. In the corner was another medical room, and the bores proceeded to wheel Mary into it.

"So, this is the Solomon Protocol?" Maxwell asked.

"Yes, a place run by the Collective. We are safe here. She is safe here. I will leave you and Augusto with her while I track down some leads on The Order."

"You want us just to stay here?" Maxwell asked. "I am a little uncomfortable with that."

"Stay with Mary," Thorsen said.

Thorsen and the bores left the way they had come, and Maxwell decided to explore the room. Fascinating art and ancient artifacts decorated the walls and shelves; museum-quality items.

The doctor and nurse were bent over Mary, attending to her, when a woman entered the room from one of the wooden doors. She had long, graying black hair and blue eyes. She was dressed in a gold cloak with a cross clasp and a *C* pin on her breast.

"She must be important," Augusto commented as she walked toward them.

"You must be Maxwell and Augusto," she said with a British accent.

"Yes. Who are you?" Maxwell asked.

She did not answer at first, but then she said, "Would you like some water, mint tea, or soda, and something to eat? Jerusalem has the best food."

"No, thank you, but we would like to take a walk. We just sat on a plane for over seventeen hours," Maxwell said.

"Sorry, you cannot leave this facility, but feel free to walk up and down the tunnel to stretch your legs."

Maxwell and Augusto took her up on the offer. Maxwell was highly interested in the murals and wanted to get a better look at them.

After Maxwell and Augusto left, the woman immediately walked into the medical room and started speaking to the doctor and nurse, with her back turned to Mary, who started waking up.

"How is she, Doctor?" the woman asked.

"She will be fine, but it will take some time."

Mary slowly opened her eyes to a blurry room. "Where am I?"

The woman placed her hand on Mary's forehead. "You are in a facility run by the Collective. Your dad, Augusto, and Maxwell are close by."

Mary's vision was not improving. She closed her eyes again. "Who are you? Do I know you? Your accent is British."

The woman glanced at the doctor, who shook his head.

"I run this facility. You are in great hands. Now get some rest. I will let Maxwell and Augusto know you are awake."

The woman left the medical room then sat down on the couch. Tears welled up in her eyes as she silently cried. The rush of emotional pain overtook her.

She wanted to tell Mary how she had to leave her when she had been a little girl and that she'd had no choice. She wanted to ask for her forgiveness. She wanted to hug her and tell her that she loved her. She was angry at the Collective, she was angry at the situation, and she was angry about who she was and who she was expected to be. Most of all, she was angry that being a mum had never been one of her choices.

Chapter 41

AWAKE

The nurse exited the medical room. "*Madame*, Mary would like to speak with you."

The woman rose from the couch and walked into the medical room. Mary was half-sitting up in the bed, her eyes wrapped to prevent the head pain from the room's bright lights as she recovered.

"Good morning, Mary."

"Good morning. I think I know your voice. It sounds familiar," Mary said. "Who are you?"

"Mary … for years, I have been waiting for this moment, often thinking it would never happen. It has played over in my mind every day, and finally, you are here, my precious, beautiful daughter." Her voice cracked as she spoke, and Mary sensed that she was crying. The woman could no longer wait to tell her. "Mary, I am your mum."

"What?" Mary said, shocked and confused. "My mum?"

"Yes, Mary, I am your mum."

Mary pulled the bandage off from her eyes with a shaking hand. She squinted hard and placed her hand on her forehead to shield the light and see the woman standing at the end of her bed. Her eyes slowly adjusted.

She could not believe it. Tears filled her eyes as the woman came into focus. It was her. It was her mum. She was as beautiful as she remembered.

Mary could not speak, trying to take in what she was seeing. A wave of mixed emotions engulfed her entire body. Love and anger rose to the top, intertwined.

The woman walked over to the side of the bed and leaned over to reassure her. "I know, I know. I had no choice, I had no choice. Please, forgive me."

Mary could see the love and empathy in her tear-filled eyes.

"I am so very sorry," her mum whispered in her ear, over and over, as she gave her a long hug.

Mary felt herself withdraw.

"You left me when I was a little girl. You left me," Mary said, still in shock.

"I had no choice. The Collective left me no choice. They said it was for your own good, for your safety. I fought for you. I tried to leave the Collective because of you. They were too powerful, and they said that was impossible because of who I am."

The woman could see Mary's blood pressure rising on the monitor. "I should go."

"No, stay. I want to get up. Where are Maxwell and Augusto?"

Mary looked at the nurse. "Can I get out of bed?"

She nodded.

"They left to stretch their legs after the long flight."

"I need them. Nurse, can you find them and let them know I am awake?"

The nurse walked out of the room.

Mary stood up and took a few steps. Her mum grabbed her elbow to steady her.

Mary looked over at her, still in disbelief. "Did Dad know you were here?"

"He knew I was in Israel, but he could not tell anyone."

"Why? I feel betrayed. Do you have any idea how hard it was growing up without a mum and a withdrawn dad? You ruined us. You ruined our family."

"Mary, I did not have a choice. They made me leave in haste. I tried to contact you, but they said it would put you at risk. I was not even allowed to contact your dad until a year passed. I am so hurt. You have no idea the pain I carry inside. It radiates through my heart and soul every day. I did not ask for this. I did not choose to be a descendent of Mary, the mother of Jesus."

Mary looked at her. "Neither did I, neither did I."

"Nevertheless, it is who we are, our destiny, and we have a higher purpose," her mum said.

"Do you remember when we were in the garden in Southwold? I knew that the day would come that I had to leave you and your dad, but I did not have the heart to tell you. I just couldn't. I love you more than anything on this Earth, unconditionally. Please, try to understand."

Maxwell and Augusto jogged into the room and hugged Mary at the same time.

"We were so worried about you."

"I am so sorry, Mary. I failed to prevent the attack. I failed you," Augusto said, looking down and avoiding eye contact.

Mary grabbed Augusto's hand. "No. You may not understand this, but you succeeded. You were not supposed to avert the attack. You were not supposed to save me from the blow. It is my path, and everything that happens to me is part of this pilgrimage."

Mary was surprised at what she had just said, but she now understood it.

Chapter 42

REVELATIONS

Mary saw her dad enter the room with two bores in tow.

"I am so happy you are awake and okay. I love you so much. I am so sorry," he said as he gave her a long hug.

Maxwell and Augusto stood nearby. Everyone had so many questions.

"Let's prepare dinner, and then talk about all this. Food warms the heart," her mum said with a smile as she walked over to an intercom on the wall and spoke.

Mary noticed that a table near the wall was already set with dishes and silverware. Soon, three women in royal blue cloaks entered the room from a side door and began setting down large bowls and plates of all the delicacies that Jerusalem had to offer. It was a kaleidoscope of colors with assorted beans and olives, hummus, falafel, tahini, baba ganoush, latkes, kebabs, salad, and piles of lafa and unleavened bread. The smell of Mediterranean spices filled the air. The food smelled delicious.

Her mum walked back to where everyone was standing around Mary. "Please, come and sit. We have so much to talk about." She motioned everyone toward the table.

Mary noticed that she had tears in her eyes as her mum sat down at the head. Her dad sat to her mum's right, and she sat to her mum's left, across from him.

"Let's pray," her mum said as everyone grabbed each other's hands and bowed.

When the prayer ended, Mary noticed that her dad and mum still held hands. She looked away with some resentment but wished more than anything for hope and love in her heart.

The pain of profound loss was still within her. It had always been since that fateful day when her mum had vanished. She was unsure how to quell it. She knew it was going to take a lot of time. Having intense love for Maxwell helped.

Everyone at the table was silent.

"Well, I guess you are wondering why I vanished so many years ago and why I never contacted you. However, I do not know if it is important now. So, I ask for your forgiveness and want you to know that it was beyond my control." She looked directly at Mary. "I fought hard for you and your dad to join me. I was unsuccessful. But I have kept watch over you, as the Alpha of the Collective for many years. Truthfully, the reports relayed back to me from the endeavor were filled with heartbreak and happiness. Can you understand that? We must now spend time together to heal us both."

"We must prepare to travel back to the States soon," her dad said as he took an unleavened bread.

"Yes, we will return after we make a stop in England, at your childhood home. I have sent protectors to scope out the situation ahead of us. It has been vacant for so long, except for a caretaker, that I do not think it receives much interest," her mum said.

Mary perked up. "We still have my childhood home?"

"Yes. We have kept it all these years for an anticipated return. It is as lovely as we left it."

"This is a lot. Maxwell, can we take a walk?" Mary asked as she stood up to leave the table.

"Sure." Maxwell stood up and grabbed Mary's hand to lead her into the entrance tunnel.

Augusto kept eating.

"I feel so betrayed by my mum and dad, but the feeling is now being replaced with an inner peace, and flashes of the word *forgiveness* are filling my head. It is really strange. The pain I had over all these years is subsiding. It is a blessing."

When they walked back to the room, the table was now filled with local desserts.

"Come enjoy some *ashishot*, a biblical dessert," her mum said as she walked over with two cups of coffee. "Coffee for you, Mary and Maxwell?"

"Sure."

Her mum placed the coffees in front of them then sat back down at the table.

"Mary and Maxwell, I have been thinking about all that has happened and the brutality of the attack. Mary, with modern technological communications, it will be very hard to be who you are, who you are meant to be. It is not like ancient times when Mary and Jesus were surrounded by followers in a particular village. The spoken word is now boundless, unconstrained by word of mouth and one's travels. Your words will now travel across all land and sea barriers and reach countless lives, young and old. As you find yourself, your message will soon become clearer and integral to moving humanity forward, to enlighten them on unity, galvanize us, and resist separatists and ideological thinking that divide us, to pick up where Jesus left off. The message could not be more needed, timelier.

"But our gifts from God come with a cost. Wherever you go, you will eventually be found and surrounded by hopeful people who are seeking your divine light, your inner peace, and your unadulterated power. Some will want you all to themselves, to know you, and even enslave you. And there will be those who just want to hurt you, to take you from us to move their agendas ahead—fear, suppression, and power.

"My dear daughter, you are the one the world has been waiting for, the Mary the scriptures wrote of, and that civilizations, for centuries, hoped for—the one who will one day walk this Earth again.

"I will allow you to return to the States, but you and Maxwell will need to remain out of sight for many months. Something is happening now, something larger than all of us, a convergence that we are just beginning to understand. You are not a prisoner, but you cannot contact anyone on Long Island. It could put your loved ones in danger. Your dad will always be nearby. In time, I will join you. Do you understand?"

"Yes," Mary said.

"Live your life and enjoy it together, for everything will soon change. This time will allow you to grow into your power, Mary, to receive guidance and messages from God. I have arranged a Collective safe house owned by a church located within Rhode Island."

Mary and Maxwell looked at each other in disbelief.

"I did not want to isolate you in a cabin in some rural place; it would not be healthy. You are both young, and your relationship is just starting. That is why I decided to send you to an urban setting with a young vibe that I think you will enjoy. You will have the full support of the Collective. Anything you need, just ask. They will always be nearby, watching. Augusto can join you, if he wishes. I can arrange a second apartment."

"Augusto?" Mary asked.

"Absolutely. I would love to join you," Augusto replied.

"It is done then." Her mum stood up and walked over to Mary and Maxwell, giving them both a kiss on their foreheads. Then she grabbed Mary by the hand.

"Now, if you will excuse us. Mary and I have some catching up to do." She led Mary out of the room. "You will leave in the morning."

***

The jet landed at the Richmond Airport just outside Newport, Rhode Island. Maxwell and Mary were excited to be back, knowing there seemed to be a connection to where this all started. It was familiar—the bridge, the city, the feel.

Maxwell did not ask Mary what she had discussed with her mum, but she seemed happy and peaceful. She smiled much more often.

"I cannot believe we are here again," Mary said, breathing in the warm, summer air. "This is not a coincidence."

"I agree. They knew we were here before."

"I am so excited to pick up where we left off. I can feel this place in my soul. There is something here I cannot explain."

They stepped into the apartment that was just a short drive from Touro Park. It was lovely, full of bright light.

"Let's go see the tower tonight. It is close by."

"Sure," Maxwell responded.

Later that night, in the security of darkness, Maxwell and Mary drove to Newport Tower in a car that the Collective had provided.

Mary hopped the black iron fence and placed her hand on the tower. An energy-filled her. She smiled, knowing that great things were to come.

Chapter 43

ORION

Mary sat on the couch in the new apartment and stared at the computer with focus and determination, only pausing to take sips of her peach tea. She had a feeling that there was much more to the tower than everyone had ever realized; a structure that might contain holy and cosmic knowledge.

"Use your ability, Mary. I believe in you," Maxwell said as he leaned over and placed a kiss on her forehead. Then he sat down at the small dinette and continued to type his thesis on his laptop. He did not get far when Mary interrupted him.

"Maxwell! Oh my God, oh my God!"

"Yes?" Maxwell replied.

"I think I see Orion's Belt on the tower." She immediately got up from the couch to where Maxwell was sitting. "Look at these three white stones. Remember how the knight's helmet was a white stone not consistent with the darker ones around him? This is the same build. I think these three white stones represent *Mintaka*, *Alnilam*, and *Alnitak*. Look at their alignments and positions." Mary picked up her phone and typed in *Orion's Belt*. She then picked an image and compared the alignment and position of the stars to the features of the tower. "These stones represent Orion's Belt."

Photograph of Newport Tower stonework showing Orion's Belt and window alignments.
M. B. Terry

"This is hard to believe, but you are right," Maxwell said, looking at her computer screen.

"Now, where is the rest of the constellation? I bet this is a marker." Mary continued to stare at the screen a little longer. "Look at how these windows are misaligned around Orion's Belt; some large and others small. Do you think they could represent the other stars in the Orion constellation?" Mary pointed to the small and large windows placed around the tower. "These small windows make little sense where they are positioned. What do you think?"

Maxwell now stood close behind her as she traced the stars of the constellation then transferred the movement to the photo. She named the stars as she traveled her finger over them.

"*Mintaka, Alnilam, Alnitak, Rigel, Saiph, Bellatrix, Meissa,* and *Betelgeuse*. These windows of the tower are in the positions of the stars in the constellation; there is no doubt. This is bloody amazing! But there seem to be too few."

"Look at these darker stones; they seem more prominent than the surroundings. Try to integrate the windows and the dark stones here and here." Maxwell pointed to the stones on the screen.

The stars forming the sword of Orion appeared as Mary connected them.

"Why would this tower have a large part of the Orion constellation mapped into the stonework and the position of the windows?" Mary asked.

"Let's go to the park at dusk to find Orion's Belt in the field to confirm this."

"Yes, that sounds great."

***

They pulled up and parked the car on Pelham Street. Touro Park was growing dark in the fading light.

Mary rolled down the car window to allow the warm, summer breeze to cascade over her. She could see people milling about and playing with their dogs on the grass.

"Can I see the photo we printed of the tower?" she asked.

"Sure." Maxwell reached into the back seat then handed Mary a stack of photos.

"This is the one. I can see the three white stones."

Maxwell was researching the Orion constellation on his phone as Mary looked at the photos. "It says here that Orion contains two of the ten brightest stars in the sky—*Rigel* and *Betelgeuse*. Listen to this ... '*Orion is important to many cultures. In South Africa, the stars of Orion's Belt are known as Drie Konings (the three kings) or Drie Susters (the three sisters). In Spain and Latin America, the stars are called Las Tres Marías, or The Three Marys.*'"

"The Three Mary's?" Mary asked.

"Yes."

"But, why place it on a tower then cover it in stucco?"

"That is an excellent question," Maxwell said.

"Maybe the builders wanted to conceal the mosaics and this constellation because it contains secret knowledge lost through the ages."

"I forgot to tell you," Mary said. "When I was in England, we went to the British Museum, and they had an exhibit on the Rosicrucian. It was very interesting in that there was an engraving that showed a tower being moved on wheels. I took a photo of it but did not view it again—that day was horrible, and it was a reminder. It is believed that the Rosicrucian also have a connection with the Knights Templar and modern freemasonry."

Mary reached into her pocket and pulled up the photo. "See here? The movable tower on wheels? Isn't it odd? Look at the ark sitting on top of a mountain in the background. Do you think that this tower had, or has, so much biblical significance that it was moved here from the holy land or built here as a guide to the Ark or something else? Remember we talked about that theory?"

"Sort of." Maxwell looked at the photo, but then her beauty and perfume overtook him, her attraction distracting him. He kissed her.

"Maxwell, I am serious," she said, smiling while gently pushing him away. "This may all be related."

"Let's go find it," Maxwell said.

Mary walked quickly ahead of Maxwell to the tower. The lights on the tower illuminated it perfectly.

It was now dark, so she was not worried that she was going to be spotted, harassed, or even worse. The sensationalism of her had died down as the world had moved on to the next viral video. Nothing stayed long in the world of social media. She knew that some of the people in the park were most likely with the Collective, watching and protecting her.

"Come on, Maxwell." Mary walked around the tower to find the three white stones. "Here they are." She sighed in relief.

"Yes, I see them. Remarkable."

She held up the photo to gauge where the windows and dark stones would align with the constellation. It was a match. All the stars were positioned on the tower in their relative positions in Orion.

"What do you think this all means? The cat, lion, and knight mosaics, the south window finds, and now this constellation?"

"The south window finds? What did you see?" Maxwell questioned.

"Yes, I never told you, but I found more unexplainable features in the south window. One stone looked like it represented the Ark of the Covenant. There were also two opposite facing faces, a crown, and three figures that I think are angels."

"What? And you kept that from me?"

"No. Well ... yeah. I'm sorry. The features are so unique and, quite frankly, unbelievable. I thought I conjured them up in my mind. Who would believe it?"

He grabbed her hands and looked deeply into her eyes before giving her another kiss. "We have enough to discuss, and if you think that your discovery in the south window can wait, then I agree. There is no way I am going to pressure *the one who can see*," he said with a wink.

Mary gave Maxwell a soft punch in the arm. "Okay now." She smiled.

He wrapped his arm around her as they walked back to the car.

"Hey, let's go back to the White Horse Tavern and talk further about this. I am in the mood for a fantastic baked potato. It's dark, and we can sit at our regular private table," Mary said. "Let's see if Augusto will join us. I will call him on his new cell phone."

Maxwell smiled. "Do you know what Long Island is famous for?"

Mary turned and put her finger on his lips to shush him. "Yes, I know, Maxwell. I love you so much."

www.ingramcontent.com/pod-product-compliance
Lightning Source LLC
Chambersburg PA
CBHW051424290426
44109CB00016B/1427